Healing Loss

Choose Love Now

Miradrienne Carroll

One Lily Press

Library of Congress Cataloging-in-Publication Data pending

Published by One Lily Press
Aloha Services
P.O. Box 300936
Houston, Texas 77230
www.alohaservices.org
www.healingloss.biz

The ideas expressed herein are those of the author and do not reflect the views of the Foundation for Inner Peace, other publishers of *A Course in Miracles,* or the Shanti Christo Foundation. The intent of the author is to offer general spiritual information to help you in your quest for emotional and spiritual well-being. In the event you use any of the information in this book, which is your constitutional right, the author and the publisher assume no responsibility for your actions.

Cover Image "One Truth" by Daniel B. Holeman

ISBN 13: 978-1456360351

ISBN 10: 1456360353

Dedication

With love and gratitude, I dedicate *Healing Loss* to my holy teachers—each and every person who has seemed to cause me loss. And to the soul I knew as Lee, who inspired me to persevere in bringing this book into being. May Lee's struggle thus bring healing to many.

Acknowledgements

Messages of healing have come to me from many sources and individuals—far too many to mention here. I give thanks for every last one. I also extend my deepest gratitude to:

- ♥ The early "pioneers"—those souls who allowed the Course to come through them, dedicated themselves to making it available, and practiced/taught what it says: Helen Schucman, William Thetford, Kenneth Wapnick, Judith Skutch, and Jon Mundy.
- ♥ Course teachers of particular influence to me: Pat Mack, Michael Mirdad, Jon Mundy, Gary Renard, Jerry Stefaniak, Kenneth Wapnick, and Marianne Williamson.
- ♥ Lynne Matous, Teacher of God, for impeccable, informed, insightful, inspired editing and the immense love that is her heart.
- ♥ Gregg Matous for perceptive proofreading with the "eyes of Christ."
- ♥ The two Elizabeths—Elizabeth Picone and Elizabeth-Hope—and Sat-Siri, Nick Arandes, and Robin Rose for relaying my angels' messages about publishing.
- ♥ Doug Thompson and Miracles in Action Press for the invaluable service of providing Urtext and Bible concordances.
- ♥ Francene Hart and Daniel B. Holeman for sharing the vibration of healing through art.
- ♥ Lizz and Ryan, angels of technical support.
- ♥ All the preview readers.
- ♥ Sally, Elaine, Kate, Kathay, Nancy, Francie, Leslie W., Bonnie G., T.R., Bonnie C., my parents, and my biological and spiritual families for their loving support.
- ♥ Michael Mirdad, inspiring teacher and gifted healer.

Thank God for forgiveness! Thanks to all who are willing to try another way.

> *Christ's Second Coming, which is sure as God, is merely the correction of mistakes, and the return of sanity. . . the willingness to let forgiveness rest upon all things without exception and without reserve. . . . Pray that the Second Coming will be soon, but do not rest with that. It needs your eyes and ears and hands and feet. It needs your voice. And most of all it needs your willingness.*
> (Workbook, Part II, 9. "*What is the Second Coming?*")

> *Forgiveness is the final goal of the curriculum. It paves the way for what goes far beyond all learning. . . . Forgiveness is its single aim, at which all learning ultimately converges.*
> (Manual for Teachers, "*What are the Characteristics of God's Teachers?*")

Forgiveness Prayer

Let my love grow deeper,
as endless as the All of You,
Forgiving as a river,
always flowing, never through,
Flowing clean and pure,
washing my mistakes,
let me love like You.

Let my love grow deeper,
as changeless as the peace of You,
Forgiving as a river,
always loving, never through,
Loving clean and pure,
loving all mistakes,
let me love like You.

Let my love grow deeper.

Protect all things you value by the act of giving them away, and you are sure that you will never lose them. What you thought you did not have is thereby proven yours. Yet value not its form. For this will change, and grow unrecognizable in time, however much you try to keep it safe. No form endures. It is the thought behind the form of things that lives unchangeable.

A Course in Miracles, Workbook Lesson 187

CONTENTS

Healing Loss

*More resilient and tender is love that has passed through the night
than love that has known only light.*—Lynne R. Matous

At perhaps the lowest point in my life emotionally—in a state of profound sadness, emptiness and despair, a depth I reached despite my extensive spiritual training—I pleaded with Jesus to give me something concrete I could hold onto to make it through the pain I was feeling, pain I expected to revisit in the days and months ahead. Immersed in the yearlong workbook program of *A Course in Miracles*, I was not sure I could stand the prolonged assault of my pain until I had mastered the material enough to find lasting peace. I was not yet having mystical experiences while doing my lessons. In fact I was often on the verge of tears, and my obsession with the circumstances that "caused" my pain was interfering with my ability to meditate and concentrate. My Elder Brother answered my plea immediately:

I'm not asking you to sacrifice. I'm asking you to trust.

Jesus' message of hope has since carried me through countless moments of amnesia when I have forgotten the inexorable Truth of Love. It inspires this, a little book of hope where none is truly needed. The Course says that we learn by teaching. I began writing to teach myself. I pray that it will help you too.

Letting Go of My Story

The loss that prompted this book showed me that it's time to let go of my story—the story that makes me both the hero and the victim in this dream I call my life. If I tell it in the proper light, I can make use of the story for my healing and perhaps yours. After that, my story is useless because, being about my dream, it isn't really true. Most of my story will not last, and the most important aspect is already known to me—my story has a happy ending. All stories ultimately end in love. Only the web of love I weave is true because only love is eternal and therefore real.

At age 50, a loss blew into my life on the tails of Hurricane Ike. Pronounced "ee-kay," *ike* is also a Hawaiian word for the shamanic principle, "the world is what you think it is."[1] To those on the path of conscious spirituality, this principle is a familiar concept expressed by many in many ways: "as you think, so you are"; "thought creates"; "mind is the builder"; and so on.

I have decided not to say exactly what loss raged through my life with that storm, to make it easier for the reader to apply the principles in this book universally. I will say this. I lost companionship—I could have lost a lover, a friend, a child, a family, a culture, or any of the circumstances that gave me access to them, or even a substance or thing that served as my companion. I lost a sense of security—I could have lost a person, job, home, culture, money, possessions, beliefs, or trust. I lost my vision for the future—I might have lost my health, home, income, abilities, faculties, a promotion, an investment, a partner, or a child. And I lost hope—I might have lost my health, looks, mind, abilities, a child, a friend, a partner, a fortune, a career, a home, a business, or even faith. It doesn't matter *what* I lost, only that I felt it was important. I believed the situation I perceived constituted a loss to me. In fact I felt devastated and heartbroken.

All of a sudden my world was no longer what I *seemed* to think it was; it was what I unconsciously thought it was—a place of loss. After Hurricane Ike, in the aftermath of this "storm of consciousness," while I struggled with the loss that shattered my hope, I realized that the emotional landscape of my entire life had been painted with agonizing loss. It was a grim realization. The loss that coincided with Hurricane Ike was an emotional trigger, recalling a host of other losses I had felt, and together they made up the framework of my story.

Born the catalyst of a family that struggled emotionally, I experienced loss from my first breath. The sense of welcoming and safety I came into the world longing for were not awaiting me. Instead I perceived ambivalence. While I was surely loved and I was responsibly taken care of, I lost the warm, fuzzy *experience* of love from my parents, who were overwhelmed, emotionally shut down, and unavailable. An undercurrent of anger lingered in our home and erupted periodically. I did not perceive a nurturing emotional foundation in my family, and so I "lost" having a soft place to fall.

I lost my inclination toward playing music to the entanglement of music with our emotionally dysfunctional family and my own interpretation of that—stage fright. I lost my sense of belonging and the support of my friends when I was sent to another city to live at age 15. As my body matured, I lost the hope of love again and again by seeking it from transient relationships and sexual partners. I lost any sense of self-mastery in an addiction to nicotine and a premature marriage. I lost any traces of self-worth in the obsessions of an eating disorder. In my

---

[1] as related by Serge Kahili King in *Urban Shaman.*

"successful" attempt to let the eating disorder go, I switched addictions and finally lost my power of choice as I became alcoholic.

I lost my very will to *live* in the fog of depression that wisped and tangled throughout my clouded youth, from ages 14-22. Then I lost my sense of health in the belief that I was forever dependent on anti-depressant medication. I lost many men I thought I loved and several friends through what I created in my sense of lack. I retreated more and more into a "prison of safety" subtly drawn around myself with voluntary isolation, losing my freedom to partake of the world. I even lost the opportunity to find support in my grief by losing things I could not speak freely about. I lost the comfort of being understood by keeping apart and keeping secrets.

Of course my story is more complex than a few sentences can impart. But in the throes of the loss that triggered my remembrance of them, the "chapter synopses" of my story felt like endless black pits of utter loss—like attracting like, loss begetting loss.

Miraculously, most of these losses I also "lost" as I pieced together recovery from one issue, then the next, and the next. At age 35 I gained the greatest gift of all—faith—as I learned that God would support my sobriety if only I would ask. With that realization, I was given another chance at life.

But even after 15 years of sobriety, spiritual awareness and study, and a respectable amount of personal healing work; beneath the progress, strength, successes, and good cheer I had attained was a recycling undercurrent of loss that revealed a gaping chasm of emptiness and despair. At my core I felt alone and unlovable. I was past overt addictions, but in my healthier efforts to not feel this core pain, I had become *distracted* by desire and *addicted* to hope. I fixed my desire and hope on some "thing" outside myself, something that would validate me and all my choices thus far. I *wanted* something and I *worked* to make it happen—I had an ultimate goal. Even though I knew better, I got attached. I nurtured *hope* as I moved from micro-loss to micro-loss when I did not achieve the particular goal of my desire. Instead I regrouped, pinning today's good feelings on hope for tomorrow. I failed to remember that a joyful choice was possible that would *eradicate all loss* and all *need* for hope.

It was not that my prior healing work wasn't good or helpful. In fact, much of it was excellent. It had brought me a long way on the path of healing. But I had reached the point where I had to address my "core" or "soul" issues head on. I needed to face them on a daily basis, not *avoid* them by hopping between the hopes in my life, like so many lily pads on a pond of flames. Hope can be a defense that subtly condemns the present. I needed to focus on *healing* my innermost pain, not spend my energy trying to control *the effects* that pain had manifested in my life. This core healing was necessary before my true life (the experience "between my ears" in my thoughts[2]) would improve. Such healing of core issues is the potential gift in loss. To let go of my story, I must heal my losses. When I *truly* heal the one loss in front of me seeming to cause my pain, I heal them all.

My experience of loss showed me where I was missing the mark spiritually. I wanted to think and feel loving in the way that I understood God to be loving, to truly manifest in my being

---

[2] "What a wee little part of a person's life are his acts and his words! His real life is led in his head, and is known to none but himself. . . . His *acts* and his *words* are merely the visible thin crust of his world . . . and they are so trifling a part of his bulk! a mere skin enveloping it. The mass of him is hidden — it and its volcanic fires that toss and boil, and never rest, night nor day. *These are his life*, and they are not written, and cannot be written." *Autobiography of Mark Twain.*

unconditional love. I wanted to *feel* like a child of God living in heaven on Earth. I wanted to live in blissful Eden-consciousness each moment, not the hellish valleys of my losses *nor* the peaks of hope that defended against them. Everything had fallen into place for my healing: I had the spiritual knowledge, a clear life canvas without active addictions and pressing practical problems, and even the time and flexibility to do the spiritual/mental/emotional healing work. And, of course, I had the catalyst—the loss that seemed to break my heart.

This little book is about transcending heartbreak. It doesn't matter what circumstances seem to have broken your heart; there is one answer that heals them all. You are not alone, and you are loved beyond measure. You are love itself. Within this book I offer principles and practices to integrate into your life that will allow you to claim these truths for your own healing. They come from my studies of the teachings of Jesus as related in *A Course in Miracles* and *The Aquarian Gospel of Jesus the Christ* and as related by my earthly teachers, as well as from other universal spiritual teachers and teachings. The suggestions herein are also derived from intuition, inspiration, and Divine Guidance. *Healing Loss* grew from notes I made to help heal myself as I studied and practiced choosing love now—as I opened my grieving mind and shattered heart to the healing light of Truth.

I'm not asking you to sacrifice. I'm asking you to trust.

I'm not asking you to sacrifice. I'm asking you to trust.

A Message of Compassion and Comfort

Namaste, Dear One,

Take heart and do not be afraid, as we are holding you safe while your eyes are clamped shut and your heart is breaking. Never have we left you alone, and we never will. Did we not scoop you from the arms of death and carry you back from your folly? We did not bring you back to suffer. Keep in the front of your mind the message of love from your Elder Brother Jeshua:

I'm not asking you to sacrifice. I'm asking you to trust.

You have lost nothing! The Kingdom of Heaven is yours to gain through this trial. All that you have ever wanted in your heart of hearts will be yours and more. You cannot now imagine the joy you will live, but we can see it here where time is not, and know it belongs to you. Take it.

When your jaw is contorted in cries of pain, your cheeks salty, your lids swollen with terror and emptiness, we surround you and protect you from all that is attracted to distress. We hold you in the arms of love. We attend to your blunders and fuel the good that flows from you, which is substantial. We love you unconditionally, beyond measure, and forever past the end of time. We are here for you, sent by our Father who longs for your return.

Do not terrorize yourself with dreams of hurt and hate. These are only the effects of an insane illusion and never part of you. Laugh when you notice them, and they will dissolve into the nothingness they are. When your voice falters, the Choir of Angels sings for you. When you feel cast away, grace caresses you.

Be still, beautiful child. Rest, and fret not. Go where you are led, and do what is in front of you. Smile and love and laugh. Dance and sing! Play! Let go of the details. You are in good hands, and all has been arranged for your greatest benefit and the greatest benefit of all involved. Everyone wins. Trust that. Trust in God.

With Abundant Love, in Service to the One,

Your Guardian Angels

~ ~ ~

Healing Exercise:

Take a moment to focus on your loss and all you have been going through. Ask for Divine Guidance, then let God, Buddha, Jesus, Krishna, The Holy Spirit, Mohammed, Mother Mary, The Great Mother, your Guardian Angels or any Servant of the Light write a message of compassion and comfort to you, *through you*. Just relax and let the words flow. You can do this. Beings of Light are supporting you right now, and they will share their love and wisdom if you ask and open to receive.

TOUCHSTONES FOR HEALING LOSS
Concepts and Practices to Choose Love Now

Forgiveness ends all suffering and loss. (Lesson 249)[3]

1. Spiritual Issue – *I am spirit.* (Lesson 97)

2. Responsibility – I forgive everything because I make the world as I would have it. (Lesson 188)

3. Support and Service – *God's Voice speaks to me all through the day.* (Lesson 49)

4. Pray – *I call upon God's Name and on my own.* (Lesson 183)

5. Meditate – *In quiet I receive God's Word today.* (Lesson 125)

6. Pain – *Joy is just, and pain is but the sign you have misunderstood yourself.* (Lesson 101)

7. Anger and Forgiveness – *Let me remember I am one with God, at one with all my brothers and my Self, in everlasting holiness and peace.* (Lesson 124)

8. Past and Future – *I loose the world from all I thought it was.* (Lesson 132)

9. Emotional Healing Work – *I am as God created me. I am God's Son. Today I lay aside all sick illusions of myself, and let my Father tell me Who I really am.* (Lesson 120)

10. Mental Healing Work – *I am determined to see things differently.* (Lesson 21)

11. Pause – *I will step back and let Him lead the way.* (Lesson 155)

12. Refill – *I am as God created me. I will remain forever as I was, created by the Changeless like Himself. And I am one with Him, and He with me.* (Lesson 112)

13. Balance – Balance is the sustenance of peace.

14. Comfort – *You do not walk alone. God's angels hover near and all about. His Love surrounds you, and of this be sure; that I will never leave you comfortless.* (Workbook Epilogue)

15. Peace – *I could see peace instead of this.* (Lesson 34)

16. Beauty – *Out of your joy, you will create beauty in His Name. . .*
(Text, Chapter 11:III.3-4, "From Darkness to Light")

17. Choose Happiness – *I share God's Will for happiness for me, and I accept it as my function now.* (Lesson 102)

18. Make Amends and Let Go – *I am not a body. I am free.* (Lesson 199)

19. Process – *All things are lessons God would have me learn.* (Lesson 193)

20. Trust – *I give my life to God to guide today.* (Lesson 233)

---

[3] "Lesson" refers to the numbered Workbook lessons from *A Course in Miracles,* Foundation for Inner Peace version, in all subsequent quotations.

The Backstory

Grief tends to wash over us in waves. When we have experienced a loss in our lives and are grieving, one of our most important "jobs" is to let that grief move *through* us. But in between the waves of grief we can set the stage for our healing. It is here that healing loss begins.

Suppose the world is not what we think it is. What if what we know and can "prove" to be "true" is actually false, and what we refer to as a matter of faith, invisible and unknowable, is true? What if the reality we know is an upside down illusion?

These may seem like questions to entertain philosophers, teenagers, and science fiction writers, but to answer them fully produces a profound effect in our lives. *A Course in Miracles* provides the information that makes these questions not only relevant but of prime importance.

Imagine for a moment God, the Creator, All That Is, the Source of Light and Life, formless, limitless, omnipresent, unified, eternal and omnipotent. Beyond human attributes, this God defines Love and Peace with His Mind and His Mind is Heaven. God extends to create a Son in His Image and the Son is completely contained within God. Oneness defines God and His Son, but God is the Creator and His Son the created. The Son of God shares all attributes with his Father, being mind, love, peace, formless, limitless, omnipresent, unified, eternal and powerfully creative. This Heavenly state of Oneness is Reality.

> *Child of God, you were created to create the good, the beautiful, and the holy.*
> *Do not lose sight of this.* (Urtext, T 1 B 40i)[4]

The Son entertains the idea of what it would be like to be separate from God. Instead of laughing at the *impossibility* of such a scenario, because God is literally *All That Is*, the Son believes in the idea of "separation" and his creative nature spins a dream about a state outside of God where God is not.

The mind of the Son goes to sleep to Reality and into the dream of "not God." And in this dream the seeming reality of "not God" is harsh, a nightmare where Love and Peace are absent. Into Oneness, duality (the idea of "other" or "twoness") has been introduced. The Son believes that God's apparent absence means he has damaged God and so into his peace comes the idea of *sin* (or "wrongness") and *guilt*—overwhelming guilt. With the guilt comes *fear*[5]—the fear that God will retaliate for the "damage" done. With that fear, into eternity comes the concept of time, that at any moment in the future God will appear to settle the score. In this single instant of deathly horror where the eternal Peace and Love of God seems ruined (*the separation*), the mind of the Son splits and offers a solution: one part says, "Let me handle the guilt for you and you will not have to feel the terror." This part is the *ego*, the part of us that finds the idea of separation not only interesting but fulfilling. The ego's fulfillment would be to unseat God from the primary position as the Creator and take His place. The first social climber, the ego believes this has been accomplished by reinventing itself from the Son of God to the esteemed author of

---

[4] "Urtext" refers to the unrevised text of *A Course in Miracles* as originally scribed by Helen Schucman. A discussion of the differences between the "Text" and the "Urtext" is not important to this book. The numeral after "T" in "Urtext" citations corresponds *generally* to the chapter number from the Foundation for Inner Peace's "Text."

[5] *God is not the author of fear. You are.* (Text, Chapter 4:I.9.1-2)

separation in a world where God cannot reign because God is not present. The ego and its tactics are insane.[6]

The ego's offer to handle our guilt involves *denial* and *projection*. The second part of the mind of the Son—the part that chooses—simply has to deny the guilt and project it onto something outside of itself. In this same moment we believed in separation, we allowed the ego to "relieve" us of our guilt and attempted to escape through projection, expanding outward in repeated separations like cancerous cell divisions, literally creating the universe of time and space. This instantaneous chain reaction was what scientists now call the Big Bang.[7] Descending further into the belief in separation caused the ethereal to densify into matter: elements, compounds, planets, and the ego's crowning achievement—*bodies* that "hid" and defined the now seemingly separate *souls* of the Son of God. It's like a "guilt virus" infected us and we broke out in a rash of projections.

Being a dream, or hallucination if you prefer, none of this actually took place. And God is omniscient only for Reality—His Heavenly Creation.[8] But the "sleeping" consciousness created by our belief in the separation was clearly distressed, so God created the Holy Spirit and placed it within that consciousness to help us gently wake up to Reality—that the Son is still safe and whole within God.[9] The intermediary between God and the Son's dream, the Holy Spirit remains in every mind that believes in separation, softly calling and waiting patiently for us to listen. The Holy Spirit is the Voice for God—the still, small voice within, the third part of the split mind of the Son of God.

Each of us together makes up the Son of God, which is why most religions teach that humanity is One. The Son is comprised of three groups in this place outside of God, our unreal world, what *A Course in Miracles* students call "the illusion":

1. The force of good, or the Light or Angelic Kingdom, the manifestation of the Holy Spirit, which retains knowledge of our Oneness with God and is helping us to remember oneness.

---

[6] *From the ego came sin and guilt and death, in OPPOSITION to life and innocence, and to the Will of God Himself. Where can such opposition lie, but in the sick minds of the insane, dedicated to madness, and set AGAINST the peace of Heaven?* (Urtext, T 19 J 1)

[7] *Into eternity, where all is one, there crept a tiny, mad idea, at which the Son of God remembered not to laugh. In his forgetting did the thought become a serious idea, and possible of both accomplishment and real effects. Together, we can laugh them BOTH away, and understand that time can NOT intrude upon eternity.* (Urtext, T 27 I 6)

[8] *One thing is sure; God, Who created neither sin nor death, wills not that you be bound by them. He knows of neither sin NOR its result.* (Urtext, T 19 J 2)

[9] *The Son of God is egoless. What can he know of madness and the death of God, when he abides in Him? What can he know of sorrow and of suffering, when he lives in eternal joy? What can he know of fear and punishment, of sin and guilt, of hatred and attack, when all there is surrounding him is everlasting peace, forever conflict-free and undisturbed, in deepest silence and tranquility?*

To know reality is not to see the ego and its thoughts, its works, its acts, its laws and its beliefs, its dreams, its hopes, its plans for its salvation, and the cost belief in it entails. (Workbook, Part II, 12. *"What is the Ego?"*)

2. The force of evil,[10] or the Dark or Demonic Kingdom, which believes strongly in the value of separation and is trying to keep us from remembering oneness.

3. The souls that densified into human form, which are confused, afraid, and creating a conflict between good and evil. Rather than simply believing in oneness (which effectively reclaims it), we follow the *thought system of the ego*. We choose to *oppose* darkness and in so doing, make the idea of darkness stronger and more "real." Moment by moment we blame outward, denying our sin and projecting our guilt. Then we oppose our projections, cementing our belief in the idea of "not God" and constructing fearful obstacles around remembering oneness. We project, and yet we do not find relief. Instead we feel guilty for blaming and project again, perpetuating an endless fear-full cycle of sin, guilt, and projection.

> *In that unholy instant time was born, and bodies made to house the mad idea, and give it the ILLUSION of reality.* (Urtext, T 20 G 8)

Keep in mind that the so-called "force" of evil is only an idea that does not have Reality on its side—it will never be real and powerful the way God is Real. But it IS as "real" as other parts of the illusion.

So we went to sleep, and came to in our dark and cold world where survival is a win/lose struggle between opponents and death is a fact of life. Our world would be like a photographic negative of Heaven, a grim manifestation of the lack of Love and Peace. But God, being inextricably in our minds as the Holy Spirit, placed a spark of God in everything we made. And so we also have the goodness of the world, the stunning beauty of nature and ourselves. In fact, *all things are echoes of the Voice for God.*[11] This is apparent when we allow the Holy Spirit, rather than the ego, to interpret the world for us. Allowing the Holy Spirit to interpret the world for us is called *forgiveness.*

The Holy Spirit is God's answer to the mess we dreamed up. Because nothing happened and time isn't real, the "problem" of the separation is already solved. We remain safe and whole in Heaven. But like a traumatized soldier with PTSD (Post Traumatic Stress Disorder), we are caught up in replaying the idea of separation in our minds. We manifest living dramas to reflect the recurrent nightmare of separation in our minds. The pages of history are full of the archetypal stories we have told about who the enemy is, the evil he has done, and how we fought against him. The details are endless in variety, and we oscillate back and forth between being victor and victim. The hero triumphs while the villain begins plotting his revenge. The innocent are annihilated—except for the tiny seed of good the villain missed. The stories are archetypal and

---

[10] *The mind can make the belief in Separation VERY real and VERY fearful. And this belief IS the devil. It is powerful, active, destructive, and clearly in opposition to God, because it literally denies His Fatherhood. Never underestimate the power of this denial. Look at your lives and see what the devil has made. But KNOW that this making will surely dissolve in the light of truth, because its foundation IS a lie.* (Urtext, T 3 I 12)

[11] (Lesson 151)

also woven at the personal level in each of our lives. They are the stories of our joys and sorrows.

The solution and healing mechanism for the stories of our lives is forgiveness.

> *Yet will one lily of forgiveness change the darkness into light; the altar to illusions to the shrine of Life Itself. And peace will be restored forever to the holy minds which God created as His Son, His dwelling-place, His joy, His love, completely His, completely one with Him.*
>
> (Workbook, Part II, 12. *"What is the Ego?"*)

In light of the backstory, my experience as a seemingly separate human being on Earth can be illustrated simply:

> God is the sun and I am at home as part of the sun. I fall asleep and dream I am away from the sun. Now I seem to be a person standing on Earth with an umbrella, the sun billions of miles away. I block the sun with the umbrella because I am afraid of sunburn. Sometimes rainstorms and lightning rage around me. I raise my umbrella in opposition to the rain and again block the sun. I hide under my umbrella and curse darkness. When I look around me all I see are other umbrellas and I am afraid. But if I lowered my umbrella I would learn that I thrive under the sun, do not get burned, and storms pass quickly. Others under umbrellas would see my radiant beauty instead of my umbrella. I put down my umbrella and experiment with standing under the sun, rain or shine. I see a few radiant beauties around me, smiling, rain or shine, without umbrellas. As I use my umbrella less, the storms lessen in frequency and intensity. The sun nourishes me and I smile. Finally I let go of the umbrella altogether. Standing under the sun I awaken and remember I am at home in the sun.

Today on Earth the fundamental error is still separation, the idea that we *can* be separate from God, each other, or anything.[12] When we block God/Love from our awareness, we believe we have hurt God and react with guilt. The medium of separation is bodies. The mechanism for maintaining the error of separation is *projection*: we take all aspects of ourselves that we have judged and rejected, hide them from our conscious awareness, and project them outside of ourselves onto other bodies, where we judge them again, finding others guilty. Through projection we make others "more guilty" than we perceive ourselves to be—thus temporarily assuaging our guilt. However, on a deeper level we are aware of the untruth and unfairness of projection, so each time we project we manufacture more guilt for ourselves! Thus we increase our "need" to project and continue doing so, becoming more and more enmeshed in the cycle of

---

[12] *The ego arose from the separation, and its continued existence depends on your continuing belief in the separation. The ego must offer you some sort of reward for maintaining this belief. All it can offer is a sense of temporary existence, which begins with its own beginning and ends with its own ending. It tells you this life is your existence because it is its own. Against this sense of temporary existence spirit offers you the knowledge of permanence and unshakable being. No one who has experienced the revelation of this can ever fully believe in the ego again. How can its meager offering to you prevail against the glorious gift of God?* (Text, Chapter 4:III.3.2-8)

separation, guilt, and projection. As we reinforce the illusion of duality in our consciousness, we become addicted to the non-sense of projection.

The time has come for us to stop using the witness to separation—the body's eyes—to try to discern the truth.[13] We are being called to open the spiritual eye which reveals a truly unified view of the universe—an eye single for Love. We translate the separation and duality we currently see into this unified view through the practice of "complete forgiveness." Complete forgiveness involves ceasing projection and forgiving twice, first ourselves and then the other, to see clearly the Divine Love within and around us. Now seeing blamelessness, Heaven and Earth pass away and we become open channels for the Will of God to manifest through us.[14]

YOU are the work of God, and His Work is wholly loveable and wholly loving.
(Urtext, T 1 B 24c)

A Course in Miracles calls this process of seeing clearly with the spiritual eye "forgiveness" or "complete forgiveness." I use the term "forgiveness" throughout this book.

The sixth major chakra (or energy center)—the Third Eye—located just beneath the middle of the forehead, makes a triangle with our two physical eyes. This locus of spiritual sight is the eye referred to in the scripture "thine eye be single." Triangles symbolize the rejoining of separation and duality, depicted by two separate points, with a third point, God, centered above them.

Lay not up for yourselves treasures upon earth, where moth and rust doth corrupt, and where thieves break through and steal: But lay up for yourselves treasures in heaven, where neither moth nor rust doth corrupt, and where thieves do not break through nor steal: For where your treasure is, there will your heart be also. The light of the body is the eye: if therefore thine eye be single, thy whole body shall be full of light. But if thine eye be evil [veiled], thy whole body shall be

---

[13] *The love of God, for a little while, must still be expressed through one body to another. That is because the real vision is still so dim. Everyone can use his body best by enlarging man's perception, so he can see the real VISION. THIS VISION is invisible to the physical eye. The ultimate purpose of the body is to render itself unnecessary. Learning to do this is the only real reason for its creation.* (Urtext, T 1 B 40j)

[14] *"Heaven and Earth shall pass away" means that they will not always exist as separate states. My Word, which is the Resurrection and the Light, shall not pass away, because Life is Eternal. YOU are the work of God, and His Work is wholly loveable and wholly loving. This is how a man MUST think of himself in his heart, because this is what he IS. As a man thinketh in his heart, so is he.* (Urtext, T 1 B 24c-d)

full of darkness. If therefore the light that is in thee be darkness, how great is that darkness!

No man can serve two masters: for either he will hate the one, and love the other; or else he will hold to the one, and despise the other. Ye cannot serve God and mammon. (Matthew 6:19-24)

The backstory of the separation and God's answer illuminates this passage from the Bible as a prophecy for humankind:

You are a God ready to forgive, gracious and merciful, slow to anger and abounding in steadfast love, and you did not forsake them. (Nehemiah 9:17)

How It Works

Truly healing grief and loss means healing the core issue that underlies it—our belief that God is not with us. This healing is a process, played out by breaking down the barriers we have erected between God and ourselves. Time creates room for us to do this healing work, but time is not really part of the work. Healing work runs contrary to the common belief in the "tincture of time," that by allowing ourselves time and space to grieve, we heal our hurt. Then at some point, we can step back into the stream of life and the future more or less free of pain, filling the space of our loss with other people and things. But if time and space are all we apply to our grief, we ENSURE that we will manufacture grief again in our future.

To heal we can use the tool of *A Course in Miracles* (the Course or ACIM). This thought system gently teaches that we are the masters of our seemingly separate minds, which in Reality reside as One Mind at peace within the Mind and Heart of God. Ideas from the Course are to be applied equally to everything without exception, whatever your particular losses.[15] In addition, we can use any and all tools that work for us and resonate with the vibration of Love Supreme.

A miracle amounts to a change in perception that corrects error. The mechanism of miracles is forgiveness. Loss is healed by changing our perceptions. Therefore, healing loss is a miracle of forgiveness.[16]

Stepping into the process of true healing, we recognize first that we are dealing with spiritual issues. We affirm again and again our identity as *spirit*, not bodies, learning to identify with our true nature instead of the (painful) events that seem to be happening to us. We accept responsibility for our own healing, then create avenues of support as we walk the healing path. We practice service as one method to aid in healing ourselves and others, since nothing lifts us away from our pain more surely than helping someone else.

Acknowledging our identity as spirit, literally the Son of God, we use prayer and meditation to increase our conscious contact with our Father. With God at our side, we embark upon work to heal our emotions of pain and anger. We also embark upon work to heal our minds because only as we change the way we think can we change the way we feel. By releasing negative emotions, practicing forgiveness, and refilling with the presence of God, we create lasting peace in our lives. Forgiveness removes the obstacles to our awareness of the constant presence of

---

[15] *The purpose of these exercises is to train the mind to a different perception of everything in the world. The workbook is divided into two sections, the first dealing with the undoing of what you see now, and the second with the restoration of sight. . . . The purpose is to train the mind to generalize the lessons, so that you will understand that each of them is as applicable to one situation as it is to another.*

. . . The only rule that should be followed throughout is to practice the exercises with great specificity. Each one applies to every situation in which you find yourself, and to everything you see in it. . . . Be sure that you do not decide that there are some things you see to which the idea for the day is inapplicable. The aim of the exercises is to increase the application of the idea to everything. This will not require effort. Only be sure that you make no exceptions in applying the idea. (Urtext, Workbook Introduction IN3-4)

[16] *Miracles are natural expressions of total forgiveness. Through miracles, man accepts God's forgiveness by extending it to others. The second step is inherent in the first, because light cannot tolerate darkness. Light dispels darkness automatically, by definition.* (Urtext, T 1 B 22, corresponds to the 21st principle of miracles.)

Love. We make amends to those we have harmed and let go of any guilt we may have been holding. As we heal, we become more and more free to simply *be* in peace.

We affirm that we live in the eternal now, releasing the past as unreal and placing the future in the Hands of God. We surrender attachments and learn to find the peace that is always with us now.

To support healing our grief, we nurture the peace we are uncovering within by pausing and building balance into our lives. We make room in time and space for Divine messages to come into our awareness. We nurture comfort, peace, beauty, and happiness in all the details of our lives—stepping into the consciousness of the Garden of Eden that is our Father's Will for us. We make amends for any mistreatment by ourselves to ourselves, and let the past go.

We honor our healing work as a process and patiently allow the effects of our work to manifest in and through us. We begin to see the events of our lives as lessons and messages from the God of Love, gently steering us to further healing and joy. We learn to trust that the Hand of God ensures that all things work together for our ultimate good and realize that we are forever safe and loved within the Mind and Heart of God.

> *All things work together for good.*
> *There are no exceptions except in the ego's judgment.*
> (Text, Chapter 4:V.1-2)[17]

Healing Loss outlines "touchstones" (concepts and practices) for the process of walking through grief to the state of wholeness. These tools are to be studied and practiced generally in addition to being called to the frontline as needed. Invite the touchstones into your life. Looking at the accompanying artwork will enhance understanding and integration of the touchstones.

A crystal touchstone for each concept/practice is suggested on the title page at the beginning of its chapter. This crystal might be worn as a pendant (at the throat or over the heart), held during meditation, displayed in the home or workspace, or carried on your person as a literal touchstone.

> *Carrying stones in your hand allows the crystal vibration to flow consistently through your energy field, using touch to access this soothing presence. Touchstones can help you stay focused on the present moment, while eliminating fear and accentuating the positive.*[18]

Let intuition be your guide and allow the amplifying energy of crystal friends to enhance your journey of healing. At the advice of crystal healing expert Judith Lukomski, my suggestions were intuited using the Directory of Crystals from *Crystal Therapy* as a divination tool. Many crystals stand ready to assist you; my suggestions are places to start, not limitations.

---

[17] "Text" citations refer to the "Text" portion of *A Course in Miracles* published by the Foundation for Inner Peace in 1976.

[18] *Crystal Therapy* by Doreen Virtue, Ph.D., and Judith Lukomski

Healing Loss

Who would deny his safety and his peace, his joy, his healing and his peace of mind, his quiet rest, his calm awakening, if he but recognized where they abide?

. . . Your doubts are meaningless, for God is certain. And the Thought of Him is never absent. Sureness must abide within you who are host to Him. (Lesson 165)

Introduction

"Hope where none is truly needed"? How could it be said that no hope is needed in this world? Dire situations, disaster, pain, suffering, and loss seem to be everywhere. The truer question seems to be where is hope NOT needed?

Jesus, in *A Course in Miracles*, describes a different way of seeing this world—from the perspective of God or the Holy Spirit. He teaches us that the world we see and live in is an illusion and that only God's Reality, or Heaven, is real. Heaven is with God. In Heaven all is One in eternal Love and safety. Heaven is timeless and without opposites, or duality. Heaven is where God is, which is every-possible-where without limit. As the Son of God (all of us—the collective, unified child that God created), Heaven is preserved *within* each of us by birthright, as we are created in the image of our Father. In the "dream" or illusion of our separate selves/bodies that seem to be having lives on planet Earth, Heaven is preserved as the consciousness of peace, love, joy, abundance, and safety.

We can reclaim Heaven now by brushing our belief in illusions out of the way. Heaven, where all is One in eternal limitless Love, is so close only our *thoughts* stand in the way. That we seem to be apart from Heaven is actually the *definition* of the physical, yet illusory, world. The physical world we experience as real is a make-believe place where God is not—therefore not Heaven. But our "separation" from God and Heaven is not true! It is a "what if" scenario. Our separation is only the fear-based *ideas* that were generated from the single "mad idea" that there could be a place where God is not. There is no place that God is not. God, being All That Is, omnipotent and omnipresent, cannot be excluded or corralled or factored out of anything. In this sense hope is not needed, because in Truth nothing is wrong! Nothing *can* be wrong within the Love of God, where God and His Son are eternally One.

If you but knew the meaning of His Love, hope and despair would be impossible. For hope would be forever satisfied; despair of any kind unthinkable. His grace His answer is to all despair, for in it lies remembrance of His Love.

(Lesson 168:2.1-3)

However, as we seem to live in *this* world, for most of us God's Reality doesn't feel true much of the time. The illusion feels true. And in the illusion there is ample pain, disaster, suffering, and loss.

God's Reality/Heaven/Love	Illusion/Physical World/Fear
Peace	Suffering
Love	Fear
Joy	Pain
Abundance	Loss
Safety	Disaster
Eternity	Time
Oneness	Separation

True healing of loss, like getting old, is not for "sissies." The consciousness that allows us to feel a sense of loss is rooted in the world and worldly matters, and as such, it is dense and usually takes effort to change. With every loss we feel we are called to this work time and again, and we accept the challenge freely in our own time. Time itself heals nothing. Each of us must make a choice.

> *Without decision, time is but a waste and effort dissipated. It is spent for nothing in return, and time goes by without results. There is no sense of gain, for nothing is accomplished; nothing learned.* (Lesson 138:3.3-5)

Time itself heals nothing. This is the truth that calls us to our work of healing. To collapse time and save agony, choose to do the work now. As a gift to God's Son (your true Self), choose to do the work now. Healing is choosing God's Reality over the illusion. The work of healing is a change of consciousness: from that of fear, disaster, pain, suffering, and loss to that of love, safety, joy, peace, and abundance. This change is accomplished through choice, practice, will, and grace.[19] In healing we learn to choose love now.

If hope is not needed, is something wrong with hope?

Nothing is wrong with hope used correctly in this world as a temporary measure, like first aid. Hope is an idea, a substitute for the thing for which we are hoping. Hope is like a pain killer that does not address the cause of the pain. Hope is the promise of peace, not peace itself. Hope is exactly what we need when we have momentarily lost our way. Hope reorients us in moments of despair. Hope is a balm for the stranded, the captive, the hungry, the rejected, the abused—any and all who sustain themselves through an ordeal by looking toward better things to come. Hope

---

[19] If Will and Grace (from the 1990's TV sitcom of the same name) had healed their losses, they wouldn't have been so codependent and attracted such catty friends!

A codependent person allows things outside himself (people, conditions, and events) to determine his emotional state. He is dependent on relationships, even when they are unhealthy. He may vacillate between guilt for asserting himself and anger over sacrificing his own needs for others. For example, he strives to "make" his loved ones happy and cannot relax when they are not. He assumes responsibility for the actions of others, or excuses their poor behavior. He may expend considerable energy trying to "fix" things for others, or be reluctant or unable to express his own preferences. Codependence underlies a wide range of behaviors. Most of us are codependent at times. Many cultural customs of interrelating are based on codependent thinking, especially those around romantic love. Codependence is rampant in storytelling, creating opportunities for suspense, drama, and comedy.

is a peppermint mocha latte at 3:00 a.m. on an all-night drive through the middle of nowhere. It'll get you through the night, but you'd better find a place to sleep tomorrow.

To *live* in a state of hope is to move out of the present into the future. As such, it is a defense against the truth and blessing of the eternal now, where God is. Hope implies that your happiness—or awareness of the truth of Heaven, or Eden-consciousness—is not here now, thus effectively *blocking you from it*. So hope is only truly helpful as a transitory comfort.

Seek not outside your Father for your hope. (Urtext, T 29 H 8)

When we hope for (or oppose) things of the illusion, we make the illusion more "real" and increase its hold on us. An attitude of acceptance places us in the position to be "in the world, but not of it." Hope is further damaging when "used" routinely because it functions like other addictions, obscuring the truth of the moment. Hope can blot out the present like a narcotic. Most of us have at some time passed through the fog of the valley of hope, missing out on the present in lust for the future: the person shaking hands with a celebrity while thinking "won't it be great when I tell everyone?" or the bride-to-be who plans her wedding while making love to her beloved, or the graduate who anticipates the next degree while being handed his diploma. All believe their happiness will come when something they want, but don't yet have, is attained.

Hope is dope and helps you cope, but optimism is optimal.

Hope is not the same as optimism. Hope involves desiring something specific and different from what is experienced now. Optimism is choosing to anticipate non-specific, positive results.

Mastery or "Must-ery"?

Hoping is not the same as cultivating vision, setting goals, and working to manifest them—also known as mastery. We must define what we want in order to effectively use our creative nature. But this is healthfully done as co-creation *with* God in the spirit of humble openness. We define, focus, act (do the next step), and accept what happens. Then we repeat the process—define, focus, act, and accept.

1. Define—cultivate vision
2. Focus—set goals
3. Act—work to manifest them
4. Accept the results and move forward

For example, if I want to be a professional pianist, it is a given that I must practice. I define what kind of pianist I want to be and focus my practice accordingly. If I want to be a concert pianist, I had better practice a classical repertoire; if I want to be a jazz pianist, I had better focus on scales and chord progressions in the context of improvisation. I define "being a pianist" and focus on appropriate practice, then act on the work at hand—practicing. When I do this as a co-creator with God, I hold my vision of the pianist I want to be, focus, and do the work of practicing. I find joy in the process of practicing. I love the pianist I am *today*, not only the pianist I hope to become. I increase the chances that I will become a professional pianist, but I am not limited to my original vision, which may not have been absolutely correct for me. My spirit is not crushed if I end up becoming a better pianist, but not a professional one. If my teacher tells me I'm just not at the level of a professional, I define, focus, act, and accept again. I might choose a different goal for my playing, or more practice, or work to remove subconscious blocks to progress, or even a different teacher. If I cannot make peace with so much practicing, I define, focus, act, and accept again. In my openness, who knows where my desire to play the piano will take me?

In 2010 Julie Andrews, the iconic, Oscar-winning, 4-octave-range star of *The Sound of Music*, discussed with Oprah Winfrey the loss of her singing voice due to a 1997 surgery. "Sadly it was *not* a successful operation," she shared, "and I had to work and deal with the loss of the [singing] voice. But the wonder is, and it's true when Maria [Von Trapp] says in the movie, '*when God closes a door, somewhere He opens a window.*'" In the face of what "sounds like chalk on a blackboard when I sing certain notes," Miss Andrews found a different way of using her voice. Since this loss she has continued a successful acting career and published about 30 children's books, writing or co-writing 24 of them.

In the practice of mastery—define, focus, act, and accept—we let go of "must-ery" as we continually choose what is *unfolding* to us, guided by the inspiration we have received and Divine Intent we may know nothing about. As we let go of "must-ery," we let go of misery. Practicing mastery we do not hope for a specific thing, then focus, act, and accept only that one thing. Such inflexible single-mindedness has been lauded in our culture for the results it seems to generate, ignoring the tragic costs to souls that choose so narrowly, whether they succeed or fail in the world's eyes. The archetypal "failure" and the "poor little rich girl" have single-mindedness in common.

Hope Springs Eternal

A Course in Miracles employs hope in the best possible way, teaching us to align with and experience the eternal state of our birthright—peace, love, joy, abundance, and safety. We learn that Heaven is inevitable, allowing us to let go and trust, which creates the experience of living in the Garden of Eden now. And if at any moment we lose touch with peace, we have every *hope* of regaining it by simply choosing again, choosing love now.

What is healing?

> *To heal is to make happy. . . . The light that belongs to you is the light of joy. . . .*
> *To be whole-hearted you must be happy. If fear and love cannot coexist, and if it*
> *is impossible to be wholly fearful and remain alive,*[20] *the only possible whole state*

---

[20] [The mind of God's Son] *could not entirely separate itself from spirit, because it is from spirit that it derives its whole power to make or create. Even in miscreation the mind is affirming its Source, or it would merely cease to be. This is impossible, because the mind belongs to spirit which God created and which is therefore eternal.* (Text, Chapter 3:IV.5. 9-11)

is that of love. There is no difference between love and joy. Therefore the only possible whole state is the wholly joyous. (Text, Chapter 5: Introduction.1-2)

To "heal" is to make whole or sound. Healing is addressing the root cause of dis-ease so disease will not continue. Healing is like curing, rather than treating or managing symptoms. We say that a disease is "incurable" when we don't know how to get rid of it from our bodies. We might then presume that *healing* loss is impossible because, in life on Earth, loss is inevitable. But we would be wrong.

The soul of every *body* longs for healing. Healing is wholeness—the unswerving knowledge that we are spirit, not bodies—literal extensions of God sharing Its attributes. To be healed is to live consciously in the awareness of oneness with God. God is only love, and therefore so are we. To heal we start where we are, choose love now, then repeat.

Former Harvard professor Ram Dass describes the 1997 stroke that so altered his physical life in a spiritual light as "fierce grace" that provided the context for further growth and healing.

*Healing is not the same as curing, after all; healing does not mean going back to the way things were before, but rather allowing **what is now** to move us closer to God.*[21]

The path of healing is a path to greater joy. We will never be the same as we were before our losses. As impossible as it may seem when we are feeling the pain of loss, with healing we will become even better.

Healing is accomplished through the spiritual practice of forgiveness. When we dig down through all the worldly layers, healing is actually forgiving *ourselves* through the process of forgiving "others" (persons or events) that seem to have hurt us. Forgiveness is *acting* on the understanding that our true Self, our spiritual identity, the Son of God, cannot be hurt.

Forgiveness involves knowing that when it appears that the worldly self—our body, our personality, even our family and possessions—has been hurt, what is really playing out before us is our own sense of guilt *projected* onto others within the context of the illusion (the illusory world). Forgiveness overlooks what is not really there![22] Forgiveness brings illusion to truth by

---

[21] *Still Here: Embracing Aging, Changing, and Dying* by Ram Dass

[22] *. . . To forgive is to OVERLOOK. Look, then, BEYOND error, and do not let your perception rest UPON it, for you will believe what your perception HOLDS. Accept as true only what your brother IS, if you would know yourself. Perceive what he is NOT, and you CANNOT know what you are, BECAUSE you see HIM falsely. Remember always that your identity is shared, and that its sharing IS its reality.*

. . . You do not know how to OVERLOOK errors, or you would not make them.

. . . The Holy Spirit merely reminds you of what is your NATURAL ability. By re-interpreting the ability to ATTACK, which you DID make, into the ability to SHARE, He TRANSLATES what you have made, into what God created. But if you would accomplish this THROUGH Him, you cannot look on your abilities through the eyes of the ego, or you will judge them as IT does. All their harmfullness lies in ITS judgment. All their HELPfullness lies in the judgment of the Holy Spirit.

The ego has a plan of forgiveness. . . The EGO's plan, of course, MAKES NO SENSE and WILL NOT WORK. By

dissolving all impediments (the belief in sin, guilt, and fear) to our experience of being one with God now, the experience of peace, love, joy, abundance, and safety.[23] God is unassailable, and in oneness with God so are we.

> *Turning the other cheek does NOT mean that you should submit to violence without protest. It means that you cannot be hurt, and do not want to show your brother anything except your wholeness. Show him that he CANNOT hurt you, and hold nothing against him, or you hold it against yourself.* (Urtext, 5 F 11)

As we forgive every person and circumstance involved in our sense of loss, we gain peace and happiness, thus healing the loss.

> *Forgiveness ends all suffering and loss.* (Lesson 249)

> *Forgiveness is the key to happiness.* (Lesson 121:13.6)

Healing is learning how to forgive.

> *Forgiveness is acquired.* (Lesson 121:6.1)

"Personal" Builds an Arsenal

Believing in the illusion of separation, we believe in the personal, which must then be defended. It is essential to remember that nothing is personal (occurring between separate individuals), so we can stop amassing our arsenals. Nothing *can* be personal because our separated selves do not exist in Truth. Furthermore, when we are not in tune with God's love and the oneness of creation, we see only the past—judging the present according to past experience. In any conflict,

---

following it, you will merely place yourself in an impossible situation, to which the ego ALWAYS leads you. Its plan is to have you SEE ERROR CLEARLY FIRST, and THEN overlook it. But how CAN you overlook what you have made real? By seeing it clearly, you HAVE made it real, and CANNOT overlook it. . . . Forgiveness that is learned of ME does not use fear to UNDO fear. Nor does it make real the UNreal, and then destroy it.

Forgiveness through the Holy Spirit lies simply in looking beyond error from the beginning, and thus KEEPING it unreal for you. Do not let any belief in its realness enter your minds AT ALL, or you will also believe that you must UNDO what you have made, in order to BE forgiven. What has no effect does not exist, and to the Holy Spirit, the effects of error are TOTALLY non-existent. By steadily and consistently canceling out ALL its effects, EVERY-WHERE AND IN ALL RESPECTS, He teaches that the ego does not exist, and PROVES IT. Follow His teaching in forgiveness, then, because forgiveness IS His function, and HE knows how to fulfill it perfectly.

That is what we meant when we once said that miracles are NATURAL, and when they do NOT occur, something has gone wrong. Miracles are merely the sign of your willingness to follow HIS plan of Salvation, in recognition of the FACT that you do NOT know what it is. His work is NOT your function, and unless you accept this, you CAN-NOT learn what your function IS. (Urtext, T 9 C 1-6)

[23]Experiencing oneness with God while incarnated on Earth has many names, such as peace, bliss, heaven, Nirvana, and Eden-consciousness.

we and the other party see only the past. We see the ghosts of old wounds that need healing and forgiveness, called into the present for that very purpose. The past is an illusion within the illusion, so no conflict, whether we are "right" or "wrong" in its details, can truly be aimed at us.

Nothing is Personal

Whoever is "out there" conflicting with, attacking, or otherwise troubling us cannot really be seeing us, because they are not in a state of love. They can only see the ghosts of their own wounds. And our own attacks or reactions also cannot be truly personal, for the very same reason—in the state of defensiveness underlying attack we can only see the ghosts of our own wounds. Outside of the state of love, we see only the ghosts of our own wounds. Nothing that is "not love" can possibly be personal because "not love" always traces back to the original trauma of the "separation," and thus is a reverberation or ghost of past wounds. And love, which preceded duality and all thought of *anything* personal, cannot be personal. Therefore, NOTHING is personal. Everything is love or the call for love.[24] That understanding places forgiveness in the proper light, allowing us to forgive (or overlook) *completely* all the "nothing" that seems to happen to us.

What is loss?

Loss is an event that reactivates our oldest wound, our belief in being separate from God.

Like everything else in this dream world of time and space, loss is an illusion. The illusion of loss starts before birth. We lose the freedom of spirit to the confines of a dense, physical body. At birth we lose the sustenance of our mother through the umbilical cord, now needing air, water, and food from outside ourselves. Every few seconds we lose the oxygen in our lungs and need more. Every few hours we lose fuel for our bodies and need more. Physical life moves from one loss to the next, with short bursts of comfort in between.

Our response of pain to the cycle of constant loss is mostly socialized out of us (we become polite, good sports), until by the time we are adults, acknowledging the pain of loss is largely relegated to major, socially-sanctioned events. The loss of a loved one to death or divorce, for example, losing a job or home, or losing some important thing we hoped to gain (even sporting events)—all are to be gotten over as quickly and quietly as possible. "The show must go on." Yet loss is the constant companion of a body on this earth because everything on Earth changes. Every moment we lose the present to the past and the future to the now. All we ever can have is the present moment. If we are attached to anything else, we experience loss.

Original Sin = Original Error = "Separation" = Emptiness = Loss

All loss in this world is, in the most important sense, the same because it is always a trigger to experience again the original loss of the Son of God, the idea that we have become separate from our Father. The belief in the separation from God is humanity's core issue. Guilt, fear, and

---

[24] *The only judgment involved at all is in the Holy Spirit's one division into two categories; one of love, and the other, the call for love.* (Urtext, T 14 F 7)

emptiness, with feelings of being unworthy and unlovable, result from the belief in separation. Loss in this world is symbolic of the loss we all share, yet never happened.

You can't fit a square peg in a round hole

As seemingly separate individuals, we each harbor a spiritual emptiness, what we could call a "God-shaped hole." Most of us cope by using persons and/or things to attempt to fill the God-shaped hole at the core of our being. We continue to try to fit a square peg in a round hole. When that doesn't work we try different pegs—stars, moons, hearts, clovers, ad infinitum. Healing loss is learning instead to use God to fill the God-shaped hole, through the process of forgiveness.

A young child who cries freely over something he wants isn't "spoiled." He is uninhibitedly expressing his core emptiness, its fulfillment projected onto an object of desire. Our common mistake as humans is that we choose a temporary peg to fill an eternal hole, something "not God" to fill the God-shaped hole we thought we made when we thought we separated from God. When we conceived of the (impossible) separation from God and believed in it, feeling its theoretical effect, we made the *thought system of the ego* to defend against the pain, guilt, and fear that overwhelmed us. The ego thrives on a never-ending cycle of sin, guilt, retribution, and fear. For the ego this is "job security." We perceive a loveless reality where God is not present and turn to the ego for help. The ego continually tells us projection is the safest thing to do. "Attack," the ego advises, in order to perpetuate itself. And, *"Seek but do not find."*[25] So we move from childhood objects of desire and fulfillment—cookies, toys, and being first—to adult objects of desire and fulfillment—money, partners, and being important or *special*. We focus our attention in the wrong direction, blind to our true source of fulfillment with God.

Inattention Blindness

With the proliferation of cell phone use and related accidents, the phenomenon of "inattention blindness" is being studied. The psychologist Ira E. Hyman, Jr., of Western Washington University in Bellingham, Washington, planted a student dressed in a brightly-colored clown suit riding a unicycle in a high-traffic campus square. He found that only 25% of the people walking through this square talking on their cell phones remembered seeing the highly unusual clown.[26] In a similar way, our focus on the physical world and distraction by the drama of the ego's struggle for survival blind us to spiritual reality. The thought system of the ego manifests an inattention blindness to the reality of God's constant presence with and within us.

Attachment

The ego self is very attached to covering the core wound of separation in order to maintain its presence and command. Therefore, the ego self does not want us to realize that our sense of loss

---

[25] *"Seek but do not find" remains the world's stern decree, and no one who pursues the world's goals can do otherwise.* (A Course in Miracles, Manual for Teachers, 13:5.8 *"What is the Real Meaning of Sacrifice?"*)

[26] As reported in the journal *Applied Cognitive Psychology*. However, 50-70% of people simply walking alone or with a friend, or listening to music remembered the clown.

is the result of *attachment,* not the result of something going away. Oneness with God is an all-inclusive getaway to heaven—*nothing* else is needed.[27]

We experience some losses more dramatically than others because of varying degrees of attachment to the object of loss ("object" includes people). Our perception of the importance of the object causes varying degrees of our core issue of separation to surface when we lose it. In other words, the more we were able to use an object or person to mask and distract from our core issue of separation, the more dramatically we will feel its loss. Generally, we are most attached to the objects, people, and situations we "love," "need," and "like."

Addiction is a defense against the emptiness exposed by loss

The experience of emptiness—the gnawing awareness of the God-shaped hole—underlies all addiction. We use substances, persons, things, or activities to try to fill the emptiness, but these "fillers" from outside of ourselves are always temporary. As a filler is lost—as it gets used up—we reach for more. Thus addiction becomes a defense against loss, because it is an attempt to quell or obliterate our nagging sense of loss of the filler and the emptiness underneath it.

We may reach for a chemically addictive substance, such as alcohol, drugs or cigarettes, or a "non-addictive" thing, such as people, food, sex, television, internet, exercise, thinking, doing, talking, or any of countless activities in which we can lose ourselves. One of the ego's most cunning moves is "serial addiction," where a string of different fillers is used to look outside of ourselves to fill the inner emptiness, but no one thing is relied upon so much that we appear to be addicted. In fact, our fascination with the world "out there" is a manifestation of this addictive defense. Spirit safe within God needs nothing. We Earthlings seem to need *everything*.

The sense of loss comes from a decision of the mind to run from its guilt, fear, and emptiness by attaching to things that are temporary. The pain of loss is the response of an addict to the non-availability of his or her "drug of choice," no matter what form this "drug" may take.[28] The *love* we feel for those we lose is not the painful part.

Losing the experience of loss

I am sustained by the Love of God. (Lesson 50)[29]

---

[27] *Peace is an attribute in YOU. You cannot find it outside. All mental illness is some form of EXTERNAL searching. Mental health is INNER peace. It enables you to remain unshaken by lack of love from without, and capable, through your own miracles, of correcting the external conditions which proceed from lack of love in others.* (Urtext, T 2 A 32)

[28] *When you are sad, KNOW that this NEED NOT BE. Depression ALWAYS arises ultimately from a sense of being deprived of something you want and do not have.* (Urtext, T 4 E 6)

[29] *Here is the answer to every problem that confronts you today and tomorrow and throughout time. In this world, you believe you are sustained by everything but God. Your faith is placed in the most trivial and insane symbols; pills, money, "protective" clothing, "influence," "prestige," being liked, knowing the "right" people, and an endless list of forms of nothingness which you endow with magical powers.*

All these things are your replacements for the Love of God. All these things are cherished to ensure a body identification. They are songs of praise to the ego. Do not put your faith in the worthless. It will not sustain you. (Lesson 50)

Every loss presents an opportunity for the rebirth of our true identity—a sacred Christmas of the heart. It is not disputed that in the world things happen to you and people do things to you. The question is, what do these things really signify? And when you can see your projections in them, the question becomes, what are these events for—what purpose do they serve—what is the *highest* purpose they can serve? And there your function can be found.

When hurt in life, many have vowed, "I'll never do that again!" But it is easy to see that sacrificing living to avoid the experience of loss just makes more loss.

The solution, therefore, is learning to live and love without attachment. Attachment to people, places, and things (believing we need them in order to live or be happy) authors the nightmare of loss because attachment addicts us to the impermanent, which will inevitably go away. We must learn to value God first and foremost, and then the inevitable comings and goings of life on Earth will be taken in proper perspective.

I will not value what is valueless. (Lesson 133)

Only the unconditional love we extend (having received love from God) is real. Everything else in this world is an illusion synonymous with nothing. As such, it is valueless. Forgive by letting go of what you think the world should be, and the world will no longer disappoint. Without expectation and attachment, we live and love without loss. Allow God to show you how to see the world and how to love here, moment by moment. Learn to choose love now, whatever "now" may bring.

If all loss reduces to our belief that we are separate from God, then healing loss is necessarily a spiritual process. An attempt to heal without God can only address symptoms, never cause, and therefore it is really palliative care, not healing. The great value of secular healing methods is that they can patch us up and carry us along until we are ready to deal with the underlying spiritual issue, but they are never the whole answer in themselves. Use them, but don't be blinded by them. A house is not remodeled with paint and carpet alone.

In Truth, nothing *of* this world is real, or eternal. All *things* of this world are temporary. Only the changeless, God's creation, is real. God's creation is Love, and we are Love in spirit. We have the power to transmute loss to inner peace. When we value and place our attention and desire on the consciousness of God—peace, love, joy, abundance, and safety—we step into the consciousness where loss is not possible. We *"raise our hearts from dust to life,"* opening up the *"path of light"* that returns us to the *"eternal Self we thought we lost."*[30] God and God's love for us are constant. Only our perception of this wavers.

---

[30] (Workbook, Review V, 5)

A Note about Suicide

The issue of suicide must be addressed because so many suicides occur in the aftermath of loss. First and foremost, suicide is a permanent response to transient feelings. As such, it makes no logical sense. Why choose an unchangeable response to changing tides? Only when suicide is taken off the table as an option can real healing begin.

Death is not the end of a soul or its suffering. Some excellent material on the afterlife experience of souls who chose suicide (obtained through a number of psychic mediums) has been compiled in the book *Suicide: What Really Happens in the Afterlife,* by Pamela Rae Heath and Jon Klimo. Please read this book if you are thinking about suicide.

In short, the overwhelming message from souls who have ended their lives on Earth through suicide is that suicide is no solution. All problems from life on Earth are carried with the soul into the afterlife, where they are more difficult to solve. There is no escape from the consciousness of one's problems. Reincarnation into another life to deal with the same problems is swift, with the added burden of having ended one's life prematurely.[31] Suicide is not a "sin" that condemns a soul to eternal hell; indeed, it is just another problem to be worked through by the soul. But suicide is a tremendous time-waster. Instead of providing relief from the problems one perceives, the problems become more difficult to work through on other levels of existence. The message from the other side from those who have done it is, "DON'T KILL YOURSELF!"

To desire an end to one's emotional suffering and to consider that peace might be obtained in death is understandable. However, death does not alleviate this kind of suffering, nor does it cause peace. It is a very serious matter if you are contemplating either the means of taking your own life or the justification for doing so. If so, it is imperative that you get skilled help from a counselor, therapist, or medical professional right away.

On top of the fathomless sadness of loss, the guilt of living in the wake of suicide can be agonizing. If someone you knew has passed this realm at their own hand, understand that you are NOT GUILTY. Barring extreme criminal circumstances, nothing you could do or not do makes you responsible for another's decision to end his or her life. Minds cannot force decisions on each other. Each of us always can choose the perspective of love or fear from which to build our thoughts and actions. The person who kills herself has chosen fear, with big consequences. Survivors can choose love now, instead of fear and guilt.

Singer Marie Osmond spoke with Oprah Winfrey about the support she received from her son Michael after her divorce, in relation to the tragedy of Michael's suicide in February, 2010: "He was proud of me [for] stepping away from sadness into light again and walking forward with my life. And I think what we teach our children is to do these things. But really we don't teach them anything—they teach us to have strength for them."

Miss Osmond returned to performing only 2 weeks after the suicide because, she said, as a veteran performer the stage was her "safe place" and she was not sure she would return at all

---

[31] All of these ramifications are also recognized in the Buddhist tradition: *"The state of mind at the time of death is regarded as extremely important, because this plays a vital part in the situation one is reborn into. This is one reason why suicide is regarded in Buddhism as very unfortunate, because the state of mind of the person who commits suicide is usually depressed and negative and is likely to throw them into a lower rebirth. Also, it doesn't end the suffering, it just postpones it to another life."* Death And Dying in the Tibetan Buddhist Tradition, compiled by Ven. Pende Hawter, www.buddhanet.net .

otherwise. The return to and maintenance of "normalcy" is key to healing loss, not in order to deny the grief but to affirm the fact that we are still whole in spite of how shattered we may feel.

If you wish you had done more for someone who chose suicide, don't try to make up for it by assuming the burden of guilt. Instead, do what you can now. Pray for that person's living soul. Pray for their safe passage through the astral plane, and send them Love and Light, strength, protection, healing, and compassionate understanding. Remember them at their best, and forgive them for choosing a drastic measure in a weak moment. Then forgive yourself for anything and everything that ever transpired between you. You will look at these matters more deeply as you practice forgiveness and do your emotional and mental healing work. For now, choose to accept God's peace and trust that earthly life ultimately ends in joy for all.

Forgiveness ends all suffering and loss. (Lesson 249)

TOUCHSTONES FOR HEALING LOSS

Concepts and Practices to Choose Love Now

Forgiveness ends all suffering and loss. (Lesson 249)

So we begin to understand what underlies our feelings of loss, but notice that we still feel bad. *"Forgiveness ends all suffering and loss."* Intuiting and trusting the truth of that, we still may wonder how, exactly, this forgiveness is to be accomplished. As we live our lives in this illusory world, what can we do to forgive, to release, and to heal the pain we feel? *A Course in Miracles* provides direction, showing us a way to learn to forgive.

TOUCHSTONES FOR HEALING LOSS
Concepts and Practices to Choose Love Now

Forgiveness ends all suffering and loss.

1. Spiritual Issue – *I am spirit.*
2. Responsibility – I forgive everything because I make the world as I would have it.
3. Support and Service – *God's Voice speaks to me all through the day.*
4. Pray – *I call upon God's Name and on my own.*
5. Meditate – *In quiet I receive God's Word today.*
6. Pain – *Joy is just, and pain is but the sign you have misunderstood yourself.*
7. Anger and Forgiveness – *Let me remember I am one with God, at one with all my brothers and my Self, in everlasting holiness and peace.*
8. Past and Future – *I loose the world from all I thought it was.*
9. Emotional Healing Work – *I am as God created me. I am God's Son. Today I lay aside all sick illusions of myself, and let my Father tell me Who I really am.*
10. Mental Healing Work – *I am determined to see things differently.*
11. Pause – *I will step back and let Him lead the way.*
12. Refill – *I am as God created me. I will remain forever as I was, created by the Changeless like Himself. And I am one with Him, and He with me.*
13. Balance – Balance is the sustenance of peace.
14. Comfort – *You do not walk alone. God's angels hover near and all about. His Love surrounds you, and of this be sure; that I will never leave you comfortless.*
15. Peace – *I could see peace instead of this.*
16. Beauty – *Out of your joy, you will create beauty in His Name. . .*
17. Choose Happiness – *I share God's Will for happiness for me, and I accept it as my function now.*
18. Make Amends and Let Go – *I am not a body. I am free.*
19. Process – *All things are lessons God would have me learn.*
20. Trust – *I give my life to God to guide today.*

Keep returning to these concepts and practices as they are the touchstones for peace.

"God" may be used instead of "the Holy Spirit" in some instances in *Healing Loss*, when the distinction between them is not important to the meaning. But God is our Source, abiding only in the Reality of Heaven. The Holy Spirit is the Voice for God within us that sees into the dream and offers guidance and assistance, created by God in answer to our illusion of separation.

Spiritual Issue

I am spirit. (Lesson 97)

Labradorite

Spiritual Issue

I am spirit. (Lesson 97)

Spiritual Issue

I am spirit. (Lesson 97)

The body is a dream. The life I'm living is a dream. My loss is a nightmare, yet another version of the archetypal nightmare—the idea that it is possible and desirable to be separate from God.

I am as God created me.
I will remain forever as I was, created by the Changeless like Himself.
And I am one with Him, and He with me. (Lesson 112)

The solution to every problem is found in our Father, the God of Love. This is because every problem we seem to experience stems from our underlying erroneous belief that God is not with us. Each personal loss of a loved one (or thing) is a re-enactment of our core issue of loss—the belief that we have been separated from God. The sense of loss is therefore a spiritual issue. A spiritual problem requires a spiritual solution.

Ego

The Course teaches that we, the creation of the God of Love (All That Is), created in God's image, have *imagined* a place where God is not and believed in its reality. Instead of remembering that such a place is impossible we perceive this place where God seems not to be and believe we have offended God by destroying Its perfect creation. Like a child who has broken a lamp, we are in the dark, panicked, fearing retribution, and filled with guilt about the mess we have made. In our panic, we attempt to hide from God and get rid of our guilt—the hellish antithesis of the heavenly bliss we have known in Oneness with our Father.

Oneness is gone in the dream of separation, usurped by the idea of duality. Duality seems to provide a means to get rid of our oppressive guilt. All concepts of duality, such as "other" and "out there" are the *result* of our dream of separation. But because we cannot be separate from All That Is, everything that follows in "separation" simply cannot be true. This dream/illusion/idea of separation is called the *ego*.[32] The physical world, including our bodies, is the effect of our expansive, guilt-ridden attempt to run away from God.

What is the ego?. . . a dream. . . . A thought you are apart from your Creator and a wish to be what He created not. . . . Nothingness in a form that seems like something . . . . There is no definition for a lie that serves to make it true. Nor can there be a truth that lies conceal effectively. . . . Look at its opposite and you can see the only answer that is meaningful. The ego's opposite in every way,—in

---

[32] *Do not be afraid of the ego. It depends on your mind, and as you made it by believing in it, so you can dispel it by withdrawing belief from it.* (Text, Chapter 7:VIII.5.1-2)

Only your allegiance to it gives the ego any power over you. (Text, Chapter 4:VI.1.2)

origin, effect and consequence—we call a miracle. . . . The miracle forgives; the ego damns. Neither need be defined except by this.

(Clarification of Terms, 2. "*The Ego–The Miracle*")

Guilt and Projection

In life, because of our continuing unconscious mental efforts to rid ourselves of guilt, our problems appear outside of ourselves, "out there" in the physical world and in other people. This defense mechanism of thought and perception is called *projection*. Attempting to free ourselves from the pain of self-imposed guilt, we project the horrors we believe about ourselves onto others seemingly "out there." By making others wrong in this way, we seem to establish our own innocence and thus gain favor with the vengeful God of our fear-tainted imagination. Through projection we are saying to God, "Look, that other guy is guiltier than me!" However, the act of projection always causes more unconscious guilt (for trying to pin what we believe is our own guilt onto another), and the cycle of guilt and projection continues.

Projection is a maladaptive adaptation for guilt. Projection is like treating gangrene by covering it with a bandage—it hides, but does not cure, the problem. We manufacture false guilt twice: first for ourselves (over the idea of separation) and then for others via projection, making the unreality of guilt seem true by judging the actions of others in the illusory world of untrue things! And then we feel guilty about it. It's enough to make our heads spin!

Addiction

Perceiving ourselves as separate, guilty, and hiding from God, we make a chasm of emptiness within, a spiritual void, or "God-shaped hole." In this illusory world where "God is not," we attempt to fill this hole in ourselves with anything and everything. But it can't be done. Only God can fill the God-shaped hole, and attempts to fill it with anything else always eventually result in a sense of loss when that thing fails and our emptiness is once again revealed.

We long for God, and try to soothe this longing with "not God."

This longing is the core issue underlying addiction. And the *pursuit* of soothing is the activity of the ego's world—"*seek but do not find.*"[33] Our guilt-based, seemingly unfulfilled longing for God is the underlying spiritual issue for every human problem. If we truly believed in our oneness with God, we would be at peace and manifest no problems. In fact, the material universe would collapse into itself and disappear.[34] Instead we believe in separation and our problems persist, never being solved but just changing form.

---

[33] (Lesson 71) Also: *The ego is certain that love is dangerous, and this is always its central teaching. It never PUTS it this way; on the contrary, everyone who believes that the ego is salvation is intensely engaged in the SEARCH for love. Yet the ego, though encouraging the search very actively, makes one proviso; - do not FIND it. Its dictates, then, can be summed up simply as, "Seek and do NOT find." This is the ONE promise that it holds out to you, and the one promise IT WILL KEEP.* (Urtext, T 11 E 1)

[34] *. . . all things he thought he made be nameless now, and in their place the holy Name of God becomes his judgment of their worthlessness.*

Forgiveness

Forgiveness is the one solution to the cycle of guilt and projection. By forgiving whatever ills seem to be "out there," we also forgive ourselves and thereby release our underlying guilt. Comprehending our innocence, we tear down the walls we have erected to protect ourselves from our mistaken fear of God's wrath. As we choose to see innocence, we experience our own innocence, and thus we see more innocence. Our barriers crumble and awareness of God's Love rushes in to fill the emptiness we only imagined. We remember the omnipotence and omnipresence of Love and claim our inheritance of peace, love, joy, abundance, and safety.

To give and receive are one in Truth.
I will forgive all things today, that I may learn how to accept the truth in me,
and come to recognize my sinlessness. (Lesson 119)

Accept that healing your loss is a *spiritual* issue with a spiritual solution. Your healing is not about the object of loss, however lovely it was or tragic the circumstances. Your loss is the surfacing of the emptiness you feel from the belief you are separate from God. Your loss is your awareness of the God-shaped hole within you. Invite the healing presence of God into your daily life as never before, through awareness, study, prayer, meditation, and healing work. No longer is such spiritual focus the esoteric realm of the few (monks, priests, nuns, etc.) who choose to listen to the Holy Spirit's call. The call has always been for all of us, and the time has come for all of us to respond. If the focus of your life is already spiritual and you are reeling from your sense of loss, some fine-tuning is in order.

I am not a body. I am free. (Lesson 199)[35]

Much of the time I believe that I *am* a body. I spend a lot of time and attention tending to my body's needs and wants. However, as I practiced my program of recovery from alcoholism, I began to appreciate the power of my attitude, even over my own body. First I realized I did not

---

All little things are silent. Little sounds are soundless now. The little things of earth have disappeared. The universe consists of nothing but the Son of God who calls upon his Father. And his Father's Voice gives answer in his Father's holy Name. In this eternal, still relationship, in which communication far transcends all words and yet exceeds in depth and height whatever words could possibly convey, is peace eternal. (Lesson 183)

The final judgment on the world contains no condemnation. For it sees the world as totally forgiven, without sin and wholly purposeless. Without a cause, and now without a function in Christ's sight, it merely slips away to nothingness. There it was born, and there it ends as well. (Workbook, Part II, 10. *"What is the Last Judgment?"*)

[35] *When you equate yourself with a body, you will ALWAYS experience depression. When a Child of God thinks of himself in this way, he is belittling himself and seeing his brothers as similarly belittled. Since he can find himself ONLY in them, he has cut himself off from salvation. Remember that the Holy Spirit interprets the body ONLY as a means of communication. Being the communication link between God and His separated Sons, He interprets everything YOU have in the light of what HE is.*

The ego SEPARATES through the body. The Holy Spirit reaches THROUGH it to others. (Urtext, T 8 G 2-3)

have to acquiesce to my body's inclination toward alcohol. My sense of mastery over my body was strengthened as I then abandoned smoking and, finally, overeating. Reiki training (a healing method that draws and focuses Divine Energy) showed me the healing power of my attention, thoughts, and intention.

> *Bodies are made of matter. You are not a body and it doesn't matter.*—Jon Mundy

I was planning to replace my kitchen floor and had a large, heavy flooring sample propped up against the stove to see how the wood would look in the room. Forgetting it was there, I opened the oven door, propelling the sample directly onto my shin bone. The pain was incredible! There was nothing to protect my bone from the force of this hard, heavy object. I crumpled to the floor in pain, assuming I had cracked the bone. And then I remembered to do Reiki. I asked God for help and breathed deeply in and out, drawing love and healing through my crown chakra, down into my heart, and then out my hands, which were cupped around my shin. I sat and did only this, with complete focus, until my pain subsided enough that I felt I could try to stand (about five minutes). I stood up and gingerly put some weight on the affected leg. It still hurt, but I was able to walk!

Before the flooring sample fell on my shin, I was about to do some prayer work, so favoring the hurt leg, I climbed the stairs to my meditation area. I sat down, placed my hands on the leg, set a healing intention, and then began the prayer, which took about 30 minutes. When I was done praying, I stood up. My shin was slightly sore, but completely usable. Later that day, I saw two massage clients, one for ashiatsu, a deep technique that utilizes the therapist's feet instead of hands. To perform this technique, I had to push hard with both legs, and I could!

The shin had a small break in the skin and a definite lump to the bone but almost no bruising. The initial pain told me the bone was cracked. "I am not a body. I am free." But I have to choose this healing truth with my belief.

> *I am spirit. I am the Son of God. No body can contain my spirit,*
> *nor impose on me a limitation God did not create.* (Lesson 114)

The chronicle of my body, my circumstances, and my fluctuating emotions is not the true story of the real me.

> *My Father gives all power unto me.*
> *The Son of God is limitless.*
> *There are no limits on his strength, his peace, his joy. . .*
> *I am he to whom all this is given.*
> *. . . in whom the power of my Father's Will abides.* (Lesson 320)

The body is part of the illusion (the dream of separation), but in service to the function of forgiveness, the body becomes God's tool for healing.

The body is a dream. Like other dreams it sometimes seems to picture happiness, but can quite suddenly revert to fear, where every dream is born. For only love creates in truth, and truth can never fear. Made to be fearful, must the body serve the purpose given it. But we can change the purpose that the body will obey by changing what we think that it is for.

The body is the means by which God's Son returns to sanity. Though it was made to fence him into hell without escape, yet has the goal of Heaven been exchanged for the pursuit of hell. The Son of God extends his hand to reach his brother, and to help him walk along the road with him. Now is the body holy. Now it serves to heal the mind that it was made to kill.
(Workbook, Part II, 5. *"What is the Body?"*)

Recognizing that I am spirit having an earthly experience defines my priorities. Understanding the problem and God's solution determines the work to be done.

God is the only goal I have today. The way to God is through forgiveness here. There is no other way. . . . Here we can but dream. But we can dream we have forgiven him in whom all sin remains impossible, and it is this we choose to dream today. God is our goal; forgiveness is the means by which our minds return to Him at last. (Lesson 256)

Remembering my oneness with God relieves me of my erroneous self-perceptions. I am not my smallest moments, no matter how pervasive they may seem nor their seeming cumulative effect.

This is God's Final Judgment: "You are still My holy Son, forever innocent, forever loving and forever loved, as limitless as your Creator, and completely changeless and forever pure. Therefore awaken and return to Me. I am your Father and you are My Son."
(Workbook, Part II, 10. *"What is the Last Judgment?"*)

Willing to perceive myself correctly, I now have "eyes to see" and "ears to hear."[36]

Holy are you, eternal, free and whole, at peace forever in the Heart of God. Where is the world, and where is sorrow now?. . . It is your function to prepare yourself to hear this Judgment and to recognize that it is true. . . .

You who are sometimes sad and sometimes angry; who sometimes feel your just due is not given you, and your best efforts meet with lack of appreciation and even

---

[36] Ezekiel 12:2 *Son of man, thou dwellest in the midst of a rebellious house, which have eyes to see, and see not; they have ears to hear, and hear not: for they are a rebellious house.* There are also numerous references to Jesus' use of the phrase, *"he that hath ears to hear, let him hear"* in the New Testament—Matthew 11:15, Matthew 13:9, Mark 4:9, Mark 7:16, Luke 8:8, Luke 14:35.

contempt; give up these foolish thoughts! They are too small and meaningless to occupy your holy mind an instant longer. God's Judgment waits for you to set you free. What can the world hold out to you, regardless of your judgments on its gifts, that you would rather have? You will be judged, and judged in fairness and in honesty. There is no deceit in God. His promises are sure. Only remember that. His promises have guaranteed His Judgment, and His alone, will be accepted in the end. It is your function to make that end be soon. It is your function to hold it to your heart, and offer it to all the world to keep it safe.

(Manual for Teachers, 15. *"Is Each One to Be Judged in the End?"*)

God is but Love, and therefore so am I. (Workbook, Part I, Review V)

Responsibility

I forgive everything because I make the world as I would have it. (Lesson 188)

Azurite & Malachite

Responsibility

I forgive everything because I make the world as I would have it. (Lesson 188)

Responsibility

I have invented the world I see. (Lesson 32)

Many of us have been taught to feel compassion for the afflictions of others that aren't "their fault"—sickness, poverty, disability, abuse, and other difficult circumstances. This dictum implies that we *should* be held responsible for circumstances that are "our fault." In this view, compassion is often withheld in favor of punishment or consequences. But the Course shows how we are indeed "at fault"—responsible for everything we experience—AND YET COMPLETELY INNOCENT. The Course teaches another way to experience the world, with compassion as the only sane response.

Responsibility is freedom. When I accept responsibility for my miscreations (mistakes in the use of my creative power) I cease to be a victim of the world I see. I am free to create something different from a wiser place. When I do not perceive myself as a victim there is nothing to rail against. Now peace is mine and I am truly free.

*Your mind is not some tiny drop in this universe. It's the other way around.
The universe is a mere drop in your mind.*—Michael Mirdad

The universe of time and space, and everything within it, originates from our belief that we can somehow be separate from God. Collectively, we are the author of this "story" humankind seems to be living. We are responsible for the characters, storylines, chapters, and scenes. I am the author of my individual story within the collective framework. Therefore, my loss is my responsibility, for it is part of *my* story. When I accept this responsibility, I am in a position to heal. My healing is also *my* responsibility.

The power of decision is my own. (Lesson 152)

No one can suffer loss unless it be his own decision. No one suffers pain except his choice elects this state for him. No one can grieve nor fear nor think him sick unless these are the outcomes that he wants. And no one dies without his own consent. Nothing occurs but represents your wish, and nothing is omitted that you choose. Here is your world, complete in all details. Here is its whole reality for you. And it is only here salvation is.

You may believe that this position is extreme, and too inclusive to be true. Yet can truth have exceptions? If you have the gift of everything, can loss be real? Can pain be part of peace, or grief of joy? Can fear and sickness enter in a mind where love and perfect holiness abide? Truth must be all-inclusive, if it be the truth at all. Accept no opposites and no exceptions, for to do so is to contradict the truth entirely.

Salvation is the recognition that the truth is true, and nothing else is true. This you have heard before, but may not yet accept both parts of it. Without the first, the second has no meaning. But without the second, is the first no longer true. Truth cannot have an opposite. This can not be too often said and thought about. For if what is not true is true as well as what is true, then part of truth is false. And truth has lost its meaning. Nothing but the truth is true, and what is false is false.

This is the simplest of distinctions, yet the most obscure. But not because it is a difficult distinction to perceive. It is concealed behind a vast array of choices that do not appear to be entirely your own. And thus the truth appears to have some aspects that belie consistency, but do not seem to be but contradictions introduced by you. (Lesson 152)

Your loss is ultimately an issue between God and you. You are feeling estranged from God, and that is corrected only by turning to God. The way to God is cleared through forgiveness.

All things are lessons God would have me learn. . . .
Forgive, and you will see this differently. . . .
I will forgive, and this will disappear. (Lesson 193)

Learning salvages the "dumbest" mistakes. The only way you can waste your life is to refuse to learn from it. Forgiveness is learning that your perception of being hurt is not true.

Mana – All power comes from within.
—Hawaiian Shamanic Principle[37]

Mana is a principle of liberation. We often spend a lot of energy trying to change others. We can spare no expense, consult an astrologer, and set up everything for the perfect day in the perfect place. We can send out engraved invitations, hire a band, and prepare a feast. We can groom that which we wish to change with the best materials. We can put on our finest adornments and use a velvet halter. We can fill a beautiful crystal basin with imported mineral water. But the bottom line always is that, while we can lead a horse to water, we cannot make it drink. This is why the only empowering force of change is the change we foster within ourselves.

Be responsible and proactive in your healing. Make time to heal. Try not to spill your distress onto others without consent and healing intent. Healing happens within *you*, when you accept responsibility by taking back your projections and withdrawing from denial, distraction, and

---

[37] as related by Serge Kahili King in *Urban Shaman.*

addiction—those activities, people, and things that temporarily mask your pain. Others can help you get there, but you step over the threshold into healing with your eyes on God and hanging onto no one.

Emotions

Thought creates. The thoughts I choose to believe make my emotions. Therefore I am responsible for my emotions.

Guilt

If I make the world as I would have it, am I guilty for the bad things happening around me? In a word—no. We each make this world by assembling the perfect cast of characters to support the healing we believe we need. (Remember, we believe we're separated from our perfection as the created Son of God.) For example, on a soul level you may believe you need a deep personal loss for some karmic reason, and the suicide of a loved one would provide such a loss. You have an unconscious, soul-level agreement to have a close relationship with a soul that has unhealed issues likely to manifest as an attraction to suicide. In the context of healing, both of you are in the relationship for the interplay between the deep loss and the suicidal urge. You are *two* directors with dovetailing needs for a cast—a potential loss and a potential suicide. You agree to work together, play it out in improv/life, and see what happens. In fact this "bleak" scenario is actually a win/win. With enough healing, the suicide can be avoided. If not, the suicide provides an opportunity for deep healing to the survivors. Each soul incarnates with its own issues to heal, and each is responsible for that healing. Other souls agree to play the parts needed to set the stage.

Projections

Projections are my perceptions of "things" I do not want to see in myself, so I see them outside of myself in others instead. My dreams are full of my projections—both my sleeping and waking dreams. My unhealed and unforgiven issues are the source of my projections. My unconscious thoughts of self-judgment construct my projections. Therefore I am responsible for my experience—for what I perceive to be "out there" happening to me.

You spot it, you got it.—Anonymous

Projection is not necessarily literal. Projection is about similar energies. Being upset by murder does not mean I'm literally a murderer. Rather, I have not forgiven myself my "murderous" thoughts—anger in any degree, for example, or dismissiveness—making someone "dead" to me.

Two examples of projection:

1. I see a drunk passed out in public and feel disgusted by his irresponsibility and lack of control. I may have never taken a drink in my life, but I project onto the

drunk *my hidden irresponsibility*—my desire to escape the burdens of this world—and some lack of control I have experienced (food, spending, temper, etc.), both of which I judge unacceptable.

2. Someone stops loving me in favor of another person, and I feel hurt and angry. But actually, I first stopped *loving* that person by demanding loyalty and expecting proof of love. I judge my own failure to love unconditionally, project that failure onto the other person—who now seems to not love me—and then blame that person for not loving me.

Distraction

Distraction is a process of losing myself in something (another relationship, school, work, material things, caretaking, etc.) to avoid the pain I'm feeling. However, when I avoid my pain, I avoid my responsibility and the opportunity to heal. Therefore I must use distraction mindfully and in moderation. I am responsible for my use of distraction.

Addiction

Addiction takes distraction to an extreme—it is an over-reliance on a particular distraction OR a string of different distractions that nonetheless are together all-consuming. The ego world operates through distraction and addiction, and circumvents healing. I can be addicted to anything. Addiction is the antithesis of balance. I am responsible for my addiction.

Denial

To heal I must root out denial in all that I do by acknowledging my feelings and being clear about my motives—all of them. Motives will reveal themselves through introspection and mental and emotional healing work. Sometimes such "embodied angels" as friends and loved ones will tell me about my hidden motives. Unmasking denial and acknowledging the complexity of motivation is a crucial step in healing. Clarity allows me to choose to support the single goal of communion with God, where peace is found. I am responsible for letting go of denial.

Karma

My soul, my core self—a byproduct of the idea of separation—draws experiences to me because it believes that I need them. These attempts at balancing past actions transcend my soul's current body and lifetime. In other words, I may be paying today for a debt I believe I incurred in another life. I am responsible for these karmic experiences, but each one provides another opportunity to heal. The healing of forgiveness collapses time and karma.

The peace of God is shining in me now.
I forgive everything because I make the world as I would have it.
Now I choose that it be innocent, devoid of sin and open to salvation. (Lesson 188)[38]

The Course describes a completely unreserved mindset of responsibility as the *only* thing we need to do to have "*vision, happiness, release from pain and the complete escape from sin, all be given you:*"

*I **am** responsible for what I see.*
I choose the feelings I experience,
and I decide upon the goal I would achieve.
And everything that seems to happen to me
I ask for, and receive as I have asked.

Deceive yourself no longer that you are helpless in the face of what is done to you. Acknowledge but that you have been mistaken, and all effects of your mistakes will disappear.   (Text, Chapter 21:II.2.1-7)

---

[38] Adapted from, "*We will forgive them all, absolving all the world of what we thought it did to us. For it is we who make the world as we would have it. Now we choose that it be innocent, devoid of sin, and open to salvation.*" (Lesson 188)

Support and Service

God's Voice speaks to me all through the day. (Lesson 49)

Tiger's-eye

Support and Service

God's Voice speaks to me all through the day. (Lesson 49)

Support

God is my refuge and security. (Lesson 261)

"Who walks with me?" This question should be asked a thousand times a day, till certainty has ended doubting and established peace. . . . I walk with God in perfect holiness. (Lesson 156)

Nothing can destroy my peace of mind because God goes with me wherever I go. . . . [This] idea will eventually overcome completely the sense of loneliness and abandonment all the separated ones experience.* (Lesson 41, revised to first person)

The truth is, all the support we will ever need is with each of us right now because God is always with us. God's Love is made manifest in this world through all life. That means there's plenty to pick from! Everything needed to support our highest good will come to us. This truth is hard to fathom when we are heartbroken by experiences of loss, but it is no less true. Choosing love now—healing by letting go of the *"blocks to the awareness of love's presence,"*[39] transforms this truth into tangible experience. But while we are healing, most of us also benefit from support in the form of understanding and sensitive people.

A runner's story illustrates just how important support can be. Determined to run his first half marathon, a man continued to train despite pain in his legs (against better judgment, as he risked injuring himself). On race day the pain was still present—he just had to endure it longer than in his training runs. His pain was so intense in the last miles of the race that it was all he could do not to give up and stop. Only the cheers of the crowd lined up all along the route, who called out to him by name (the runners' names were clearly printed on their backs), gave him the extra grit and determination he needed to finish his race.

Don't try to run this race on your own. If you're tempted, remember the old song:

"I am strong! I am invincible! I'm Atlantis!"

Spiritual Focus

Seek support and comfort from others who understand the spiritual nature of your struggle and the sacred importance and difficulty of your task. If you are depressed, without supportive people in your life, have a great deal of loss or very serious loss to process, then work with a counselor and/or grief support group.[40] It is cleansing, empowering, and comforting to have an opportunity to express your feelings in an environment of understanding, love, and acceptance.

If none practice in your area, many counselors who base their work on the principles of *A Course in Miracles* (ACIM) are available for phone sessions.

---

[39] Introduction to *A Course in Miracles*, Foundation for Inner Peace

[40] If you have lost a child, for example, connect with The Compassionate Friends, www.compassionatefriends.org . Online support is available for numerous kinds of loss at www.griefnet.org .

- Jon Mundy's *Miracles* magazine features articles, ads for counseling services, and a listing of major teachers and groups. www.miraclesmagazine.org

- Miracle Distribution Center maintains a directory of therapists, counselors, and coaches whose practices draw from the wisdom of ACIM. www.miraclecenter.org

Avoid seeking advice from those who see your issues only in worldly terms, as this will reinforce illusions when you are vulnerable to believing them and delay your healing. Share love and companionship with them, but do not rely on them for direction in healing your pain.

At some point well into your healing process you may benefit from a psychic or angel reading from a reputable practitioner. I advise getting a personal recommendation—mine is Elizabeth Picone.[41] Approach readings with openness, and be mindful not to use them to avoid mental and emotional healing work, making your own decisions in life, or developing your own intuition. Readings are just another resource among many.

Patience

Beware of urges to replace your loss too soon. If your loss is an intimate relationship, wait at least a year and quite possibly longer before seeking another. It is important that you acknowledge your emptiness and pause within it, allowing space for healing and Divine Guidance. Seeking relief in relationships courts codependency, and codependency halts healing in the same way as other active addictions.[42] Enjoy friendships, focus on your healing work, take things slowly, and wait to enter more serious relationships.

Moderation

Beware of seeking peace through distraction too often. The time for healing is now, and your task is at hand. You have been called. This is not to say that you can't travel, take a class, watch TV, work hard or go out and have fun. Just understand that all of these things, and many more, *can* be employed as distractions from your pain and the work that heals it, so don't overdo them now. This goal of moderation also applies to service.

---

[41] www.elizabethpicone.com

[42] *Seek not outside yourself. For it will fail, and you will weep each time an idol falls. Heaven cannot be found where it is not, and there can be no peace EXCEPTING there. Each idol that you worship when God calls will never answer in His place. There IS no other answer you can substitute, and find the happiness His Answer brings. Seek not outside yourself. For all your pain comes simply from a futile search for what you want, insisting WHERE it must be found. What if it is not there? Do you prefer that you be right or happy? Be you glad that you are told where happiness abides, and seek no longer elsewhere. You will fail.* (Urtext, T 29 H 1)

Service

For the greater individual is the one who is the servant of all. And to conquer self is greater than taking many cities. For, here ye may find humbleness as against that which cries oft for expression, and the feeling of not being appreciated. Express it more in the greater amount of love upon those who may be aided through thy effort. For, remember, man looks upon the things of the day but God looks upon the heart.

(Edgar Cayce Reading 3253-2)

I bless the world because I bless myself. (Lesson 187)

. . . you do not lack for proof that when you give ideas away, you strengthen them in your own mind. . . . Ideas must first belong to you, before you give them. If you are to save the world, you first accept salvation for yourself. But you will not believe that this is done until you see the miracles it brings to everyone you look upon. . . .

Protect all things you value by the act of giving them away, and you are sure that you will never lose them. What you thought you did not have is thereby proven yours. Yet value not its form. For this will change, and grow unrecognizable in time, however much you try to keep it safe. No form endures. It is the thought behind the form of things that lives unchangeable. . . .

Never forget you give but to yourself. Who understands what giving means must laugh at the idea of sacrifice. Nor can he fail to recognize the many forms which sacrifice may take. He laughs as well at pain and loss, at sickness and at grief, at poverty, starvation and at death. He recognizes sacrifice remains the one idea that stands behind them all, and in his gentle laughter are they healed.

Illusion recognized must disappear. Accept not suffering, and you remove the thought of suffering. Your blessing lies on everyone who suffers when you choose to see all suffering as what it is. The thought of sacrifice gives rise to all the forms that suffering appears to take. And sacrifice is an idea so mad that sanity dismisses it at once.

Never believe that you can sacrifice. There is no place for sacrifice in what has any value. If the thought occurs, its very presence proves that error has arisen, and correction must be made. Your blessing will correct it.

(Lesson 187)

Inherent in the idea of sacrifice is the belief that you can be a victim. But a creator cannot also be a victim. And since you always receive as you give, you cannot "sacrifice" anything.

Support yourself through service to others. Your own healing is service to others.[43] Service is also anything you do with love, great or small, for the benefit of someone else. It may take a few minutes or become the largest part of your life. It doesn't matter. *All expressions of love are maximal.*[44]

> *I offer only miracles today, for I would have them be returned to me. . . . And every one I give returns to me, reminding me the law of love is universal. . . . The miracles I give are given back in just the form I need to help me with the problems I perceive.*   (Lesson 345)

Always serve from a secure footing in God's reality of peace, love, joy, abundance, and safety. From your place of balance on this "rock" you can reach into areas of need, even the pain and chaos of others' traumas, to assist them in finding a foothold on the "rock" themselves.

> *Let my mind be healed, that I may carry healing to the world.*[45]
> Let only truth occupy my mind.[46]
> *When I am healed I am not healed alone.*[47]

The following lesson applies to service as well as to healing yourself. Remember that healing yourself *is* the highest level of service. You don't have to be perfect or completely healed, but having attained a certain balance, you can safely heal yourself AND serve others.

> *I am the holy Son of God Himself. I cannot suffer, cannot be in pain; I cannot suffer loss, nor fail to do all that salvation asks. . . .*
>
> *You who perceive yourself as weak and frail, with futile hopes and devastated dreams, born but to die, to weep and suffer pain, hear this: All power is given unto you in earth and Heaven. There is nothing that you cannot do. You play the game of death, of being helpless, pitifully tied to dissolution in a world which shows no mercy to you. Yet when you accord it mercy, will its mercy shine on you.*

---

[43] *Children of peace, the light HAS come to you. The light you bring you do NOT recognize, and yet you will remember. Who can deny HIMSELF the vision that he brings to others? And who would fail to recognize a gift he let be laid in Heaven through HIMSELF? The gentle service that you give the Holy Spirit IS service to yourself. You who are now HIS means must love all that He loves. And what you bring is YOUR remembrance of everything that is eternal. No trace of anything in time can long remain in minds that serve the timeless. And NO illusion can disturb the peace of a relationship which has become the MEANS of peace.* (Urtext, T 22 G 6)

[44] From number one of the Principles of Miracles, (Text, Chapter 1:I.1.4)

[45] (Lesson 136)

[46] Adapted from Lesson 107, *Truth will correct all errors in my mind.*

[47] (Lesson 137)

Then let the Son of God awaken from his sleep, and opening his holy eyes, return again to bless the world he made. . . . join with me today. Your glory is the light that saves the world. Do not withhold salvation longer. Look about the world, and see the suffering there. Is not your heart willing to bring your weary brothers rest?

They must await your own release. They stay in chains till you are free. They cannot see the mercy of the world until you find it in yourself. They suffer pain until you have denied its hold on you. They die till you accept your own eternal life. You are the holy Son of God Himself. Remember this, and all the world is free. Remember this, and earth and Heaven are one.

(Lesson 191)

~ ~ ~

In the following story from *The Aquarian Gospel of Jesus the Christ*, Jesus acknowledges the role of service in healing grief as he undertakes his seventh initiation in Egypt, working in the hall of the dead. After advising a grief-stricken woman to *"lose yourself in helping others dry their tears,"* he notices a young girl leave the body of her mother to tend to a wounded bird and asks her why.

The maiden said, This lifeless body needs no help from me; but I can help while yet life is; my mother taught me this.

My mother taught that grief and selfish love, and hopes and fears are but reflexes from the lower self; that what we sense are but small waves upon the rolling billows of a life. These all will pass away; they are unreal.

Tears flow from the hearts of flesh; the spirit never weeps; and I am longing for the day when I will walk in light, where tears are wiped away. My mother taught me that all emotions are the sprays that rise from human loves, and hopes, and fears; that perfect bliss cannot be ours till we have conquered these.

The people and things we lose become our teachers. All that is temporary is unreal, including our earthly emotions, our bodily selves, and our loved ones in physical form. We cannot attain the consciousness of Heaven until we have let go of everything temporary, as Jesus did.

And in the presence of that child did Jesus bow his head in reverence. He said, For days and months and years I've sought to learn this highest truth that man can learn on earth, and here a child, fresh brought to earth, has told it all in one short breath . . . . And then he laid his hand upon the maiden's head, and said, I'm sure the blessings of my Father-God will rest upon you, child, for evermore.
(*The Aquarian Gospel of Jesus the Christ*, Section XI, Chapter 54)

Jesus' blessing extends through time to us when we learn these truths that put our priorities in order. My emotions about the events of my life on Earth are as illusory as the events themselves. In order to regain bliss, I must be willing to walk away from the reflexes of my lower self. In order to walk in the light of the Love of God, I must put my energy into what is true (eternal) and let go of what is unreal (of the lower self).

Pray

I call upon God's Name and on my own. (Lesson 183)

White Topaz

Pray

I call upon God's Name and on my own. (Lesson 183)

Pray

Everyone who has ever tried to use prayer to request something has experienced what appears to be failure. This is not only true in connection with specific things which might be harmful, but also in connection with requests which are strictly in line with this course. The latter, in particular, might be incorrectly interpreted as "proof" that the course does not mean what it says. But you must remember that the course does state, and REPEATEDLY, that its purpose is the ESCAPE FROM FEAR.

Let us suppose, then, that what you request of the Holy Spirit IS what you really want, but that YOU ARE STILL AFRAID OF IT. Should this be the case, your ATTAINMENT of it would no longer BE what you want, even if IT is. This accounts for why CERTAIN SPECIFIC FORMS of healing are not achieved, even though the STATE of healing IS. It frequently happens that an individual asks for physical healing, because he is fearful OF BODILY HARM. However, at the same time, if he WERE healed physically, the threat to his thought-system would be considerably MORE fearful to him than its physical EXPRESSION. In this case, he is not really asking for RELEASE from fear, but for the removal of a symptom WHICH HE HAS SELECTED. This request is, therefore, NOT for healing at all.

The Bible emphasizes that ALL prayers are answered, and this must be true, if no effort is wasted. The very fact that one has asked the Holy Spirit for ANYTHING, will ensure a response. But it is equally certain that no response, given by the Holy Spirit, will EVER be one which would INCREASE fear. It is even possible that His answer will not be heard at all. It is IMpossible, however, that it will be lost. There are many answers which you have already received, but have NOT YET HEARD. I assure you that they are waiting for you. It is indeed true that no effort is wasted. (Urtext, T 8 K 1-3)

Ask for help and guidance from the higher realms—God's Servants of Light. It is not assured that you will get what you pray for, but your prayer will be answered.

For many months I prayed daily for the healing of my loss in various ways. Most often I prayed for peace of mind, guidance, and spiritual advancement. I prayed for strength to carry out what was in front of me. I prayed to be a conduit of Divine healing. These prayers were always answered. But I also prayed "big"—for complete healing of all factors related to my loss and for unmistakable signs that complete healing had occurred. I have seen unmistakable manifestations of love and forgiveness, but the complete healing that would "end" this particular story of loss hasn't happened yet. I trust it will come to pass. Meanwhile, *my present happiness is all I see.*[48]

The highest level of prayer is communion with God, simply being with All That Is in receptive silence. The Workbook lessons of *A Course in Miracles* provide training to achieve this sacred communion. But while we are in the throes of grief, this level of prayer may be

[48] (Lesson 290)

elusive. Still, call out to God. God sends assistance to His children in distress. Clear the way. Make it known that you are open to Divine assistance by asking for help. Send your prayers of need, such as:

God, help me.

God, be with me now.

God, show me how You would see this.

No matter what we are going through in our human lives, consciously calling in God can only be helpful. Don't let any judgment about your level of prayer, or doubt about whether it will be answered, stop you from asking God to be with you in your experience. As we are able, we refine our communication with God into sacred communion.

Having participated in hundreds of anonymous support meetings, I saw that God answers the prayers of those who sincerely ask for sobriety. That was also my personal experience—whenever I prayed for my own sobriety, I did not drink. God seems to bless alcoholics and addicts who ask with *whatever* they truly need to stay clean and sober. I used to puzzle over why that is. Doesn't God love drunks and addicts exactly as they are (whether drunk or sober) and as much as everyone else? If God loves His Son, then the answer has to be yes. Isn't the world an illusion? Yes. Does sobriety matter more than other illusory states? How could it? Do we have free will? Yes—and the will of an addict seems to be to use whatever she is addicted to. So why would God so reliably grant "sobriety upon request" when God does not so reliably grant many other requests, such as "make this a success" or "heal this disease" or "fix this relationship" or "buy me a Mercedes Benz"?

Eventually, through practicing the Course, I understood. God's Will is our happiness, and to have that we must know Him. Our happiness is not with the things we think we want—our happiness is with Him. Drugs and alcohol get in the way of our awareness of God. Drugs and alcohol easily become a false idol in place of God. So anytime an addict or alcoholic uses his free will to ask for help staying clean and sober, all the power of God rushes in to support, so that the addicted person may know Him and be happy.

God's Will for me is perfect happiness. (Lesson 101)

Pray that God's Will be done through you.

This prayer is the door that leads out of the desert [the separation] *forever.*

"If you will tell me what to do, ONLY THAT I will to do."
You must be
READY to listen
WILLING to learn
and ABLE to do.

Only the last is involuntary, because it is the APPLICATION of miracles which must be Christ-controlled. But the other two, which are the voluntary aspects of miracle-mindedness, ARE up to you. (Urtext, T 1 B 40, m-o, q-r, t, compilation)

Pray to God from wherever you are—be it grief or exaltation. It has been promised that God will meet you within your inner self, where the memory of Him has been placed. Prayers of need will become prayers of communion as you heal and practice. More and more, your prayer will resonate "Here I am, God," as you silently listen.

God's Name can not be heard without response, nor said without an echo in the mind that calls you to remember. Say His Name, and you invite the angels to surround the ground on which you stand, and sing to you as they spread out their wings to keep you safe, and shelter you from every worldly thought that would intrude upon your holiness. (Lesson 183:2.1-2)

Pray simply, "God," as if no other word or idea exists, for that is the Truth.

Repeat God's Name, and you acknowledge Him as sole Creator of reality. And you acknowledge also that His Son is part of Him, creating in His Name. Sit silently, and let His name become the all-encompassing idea that holds your mind completely. Let all thoughts be still except this one. (Lesson 183:8.1-4)

Pray for release from all things of the world that hold you here. Here is a prayer of mine, an adaptation of one by Byron Katie, using concepts from the Workbook lessons:

Beloved Father, help me let go of the desire for
love, attention, approval, and appreciation.
The world I see holds nothing that I want.[49]
I want the peace of God.[50]
You are my goal, my Father. Only You.[51]

Pray for communion with your Beloved Father.

Father, I come to You today to seek the peace that You alone can give. I come in silence. In the quiet of my heart, the deep recesses of my mind, I wait and listen for Your Voice. My Father, speak to me today. I come to hear Your Voice in silence and in certainty and love, sure You will hear my call and answer me. (Lesson 221:1.1-5)

Prayers of communion naturally lead to meditation.

---

[49] (Lesson 129)

[50] (Lesson 185)

[51] (Lesson 287)

Meditate

In quiet I receive God's Word today. (Lesson 125)

Smoky Quartz

Meditate

In quiet I receive God's Word today. (Lesson 125)

Meditate

Meditation is a choice to retire for a time from the illusory world and listen instead for what is Real. God is revealed (remembered) and experienced in silence. The spiritual advice to practice silence is longstanding, widespread, and well-founded. Our churches, temples, and synagogues are, in part, refuges for the practice of silence. The simple path outlined by Mother Teresa starts in silence and ends in peace. Even when we connect with the Divine during chaos, we lock in that connection in the quiet space we cultivate between our thoughts. Meditation is like erasing a mental white board. We clear the jumble of our thoughts to make room for the Thought of God to be written. The Thought of God always comes in peace.

Be still, and know that I am God. (Psalm 46:10)

Issues in need of healing—issues that contribute to our sense of loss—also often surface in silence. Our mission is to heal our sense of loss by strengthening our conscious contact with God, in Whose Light loss is not possible. Now is the time to be quiet and pay attention. Meditation is the place where we face our addiction to everything that seems to be outside our self.

Let me be still and listen to the truth. (Lesson 106)

Multitudes on a conscious spiritual path want to feel closer to God and expend plenty of time and energy in that pursuit. We read books, study, practice, go to workshops, undertake initiations and journeys, pray, receive bodywork and other healing sessions, participate in services and rituals, tithe, teach, write, sing, and spread the good news of Love Everlasting with our joyous examples when and wherever we are able. More rarely do we sit quietly and listen to the message our Father would have us hear. God's loving assurance of eternal peace and joy awaits in the stillness within us, placed there by our Father where we cannot fail to find it.

The Course teaches that God planted the "Thought of peace" within our minds at the moment we conceived of and believed in the idea of separation.

Let go all the trivial things that churn and bubble on the surface of your mind, and reach down and below them to the Kingdom of Heaven. There is a place in you where there is perfect peace. There is a place in you where nothing is impossible. There is a place in you where the strength of God abides. (Lesson 47)

Tucked safely within each of us, peace is always accessible by "undoing" or clearing the clamor that covers it—through forgiveness (undoing judgments, which maintain the illusion of separation) and through meditation (undoing focus on the illusory world). In this process of undoing, our *salvation*—our full awareness of our oneness with God— is reclaimed.

Salvation is undoing in the sense that it does nothing, failing to support the world of dreams and malice. Thus it lets illusions go. By not supporting them, it merely lets them quietly go down to dust. And what they hid is now revealed; an altar to the holy Name of God whereon His Word is written, with the gifts of your forgiveness laid before it, and the memory of God not far behind.

Let us come daily to this holy place, and spend a while together. Here we share our final dream. It is a dream in which there is no sorrow, for it holds a hint of all the glory given us by God. (Workbook, Part II, 2. *"What is Salvation?"*)

The tangled maze of ego-journeys we might take, winding this way and that, cannot separate us further from the truth inside, just a pulse of silence and defenselessness away. When the incessant voice of the ego ("the voice in the head" as Eckhart Tolle calls it) subsides and surrenders a breath of silence to us, our true identity (the witness to the ego's voice) reconnects with the memory of God planted within. We are restored and uplifted, and gently eased toward identifying more with the witness than the ego's voice. God's Son is given *"a little time to be Himself, within the peace that is His home, resting in silence and in peace and love."* (Lesson 182:5.7)

I will be still an instant and go home. (Lesson 182)

The Course offers ample instruction on the process of meditation. For example:

Simply do this: Be still, and lay aside all thoughts of what you are and what God is; all concepts you have learned about the world; all images you hold about yourself. Empty your mind of everything it thinks is either true or false, or good or bad, of every thought it judges worthy, and all the ideas of which it is ashamed. Hold onto nothing. Do not bring with you one thought the past has taught, nor one belief you ever learned before from anything. Forget this world, forget this course, and come with wholly empty hands unto your God.

Is it not He Who knows the way to you? You need not know the way to Him. Your part is simply to allow all obstacles that you have interposed between the Son and God the Father to be quietly removed forever. God will do His part in joyful and immediate response. Ask and receive. But do not make demands, nor point the road to God by which He should appear to you. The way to reach Him is merely to let Him be. For in that way is your reality proclaimed as well. (Lesson 189:7-8)

Practice silent meditation daily. Nothing offers richer blessings.

God's meeting place with man is in the heart,
and in a still small voice he speaks; and he who hears is still.
(*The Aquarian Gospel of Jesus the Christ,* Section VI, Chapter 26:7)

Walking on the beach one day, I noticed a dog with a ball waiting at the shore in a state of eager anticipation. His master was nowhere in sight. The dog was meditating. . . . His master came.

Meditation is a silent state of eager anticipation, a poised readiness to experience God.

Jesus offers this encouragement and instruction, promising magnificent rewards:

And Jesus said, There is a Silence where the soul may meet its God, and there the fount of wisdom is, and all who enter are immersed in light, and filled with wisdom, love and power. . . .

Men carry with them all the time the secret place where they may meet their God. It matters not where men abide. . .; they may at once, at any time, fling wide the door, and find the Silence, find the house of God; it is within the soul. . . .

And when life's heavy load is pressing hard, it is far better to go out and seek a quiet place to pray and meditate. The Silence is the kingdom of the soul which is not seen by human eyes.

When in the Silence, phantom forms may flit before the mind; but they are all subservient to the will; the master soul may speak and they are gone.

If you would find this Silence of the soul you must yourself prepare the way. None but the pure in heart may enter here. And you must lay aside all tenseness of the mind, all business cares, all fears, all doubts and troubled thoughts. Your human will must be absorbed by the divine; then you will come into a consciousness of holiness.

You are within the Holy Place, and you will see upon a living shrine the candle of the Lord aflame. And when you see it burning there, look deep within the temple of your brain, and you will see it all aglow. In every part, from head to foot, are candles all in place, [chakras] just waiting to be lighted by the flaming torch of love. And when you see the candles all aflame, just look, and you will see, with eyes of soul, the waters of the fount of wisdom rushing on; and you may drink, and there abide.

And then the curtains part, and you are in the Holiest of All, where rests the Ark of God, whose covering is the Mercy Seat. Fear not to lift the sacred board; the Tables of the Law are in the Ark concealed. Take them and read them well; for they contain all precepts and commands that men will ever need.

And in the Ark, the magic wand of prophecy lies waiting for your hand; it is the key to all the hidden meanings of the present, future, past. And then, behold, the manna there, the hidden bread of life; and he who eats shall never die.

The cherubim[52] have guarded well for every soul this treasure box, and whosoever will may enter in and find his own.
(The Aquarian Gospel of Jesus the Christ, Section VIII, Chapter 40)

---

[52] Among the highest trinity of angels, the cherubim function as God's record keepers.

Especially in times of stress or when silence is a new practice, everything *but* peace may surface during meditation sessions.[53] Don't be alarmed. The voice in the head does not take well to being disregarded. The ego does not want you to meditate, but you are setting the stage for healing. Issues that are suppressed and paved over during the busy course of the day may come into awareness. Even if you experience a lot of mental or emotional chatter, take heart as you are making great progress! Use the information that's coming up—thoughts, feelings, and memories—for your healing. Do the work now. Some of the most beautiful moments I've experienced have come after doing emotional or mental healing work *within* my meditation.

Above all else, persist in your practice of silence that you may receive its gifts.

> *The peace of God is shining in me now.*
> *I will be still, and let the earth be still along with me.*
> *And in that stillness we will find the peace of God.*
> *It is within my heart, which witnesses to God Himself.* (Lesson 208)

In my practice of stillness, I experience both the pitfalls and gifts of meditation. Sometimes my thoughts of worldly matters are noisy and insistent, and it can take most of my session to settle into quiet. Most days I have to work around my "bunny mind" that hops around and likes to stop and chew on things. Often, however, my sessions are peaceful and I see colors, but otherwise unremarkable. Sometimes I receive inspiration, mostly about this book. But, ah, the beauty of the inner sanctuary when it is reached! I experience unbreakable stillness, deep peace, and Light from behind my eyes. I see colors and sometimes geometric patterns. Archangel Michael heals me with electric blue and purple pulses and flashes of light. Sometimes my whole head fills with Light. Eventually I feel my consciousness expand beyond the physical boundary of my body. I might have little dreams that make no sense to me but feel like dreams of release. Sometimes gentleness settles over me, like frost on the sleeping earth, and all the world is covered in velvet.

> *Peace to my mind. Let all my thoughts be still.* (Lesson 221)

Peace, stillness, safety, healing, joy, timelessness. I rest within the peace of God, sharing with all my brothers throughout time. Through meditation I learn that the peace that I am is my *cause* for joy.

> *Heaven itself is reached with empty hands and open minds.* (Lesson 133)

Only heaven do I seek, and it belongs to me.

---

[53] Some of us are more deeply entrenched in constant thinking and/or anxiety. In this case, "hypno-meditation"— silent meditation preceded by entering a state of hypnosis—can be very helpful. Instructions and a script for hypno-meditation are included at the end of this chapter.

Meditation Method Overview

1. Sit comfortably with your back straight and legs and hands uncrossed.

2. Set your intention to commune with God with a prayer, decree, or simple declaration. Set your intention for the length of the session.

3. Prepare your mind using inspiring material with directions, benefits, and effects of meditation. Several suitable passages are in this chapter. Close your eyes and tone[54] if desired.

4. Follow the breath. Use a mantra to quiet other thoughts.

5. Switch focus to the silence between breaths.

6. Allow the silence to take you. Feel the peace and love you are choosing. Let a smile be born on your lips. Be open to Divine inspiration and messages.

7. Check in—is your heart wide open? If not, consciously open it.

8. When you are finished sitting in silence tone, if desired, and give thanks for the experience. You may also wish to send out prayers from this place of higher vibrational frequency.

Some Methods: (especially helpful when the mind is busy with thoughts—use alone or combine)

♥ Begin with a prayer of intent, then quiet your mind. For example:

God, here I am to remember Your Love. Help me to transcend the world.

Your grace is given me. I claim it now. Father, I come to You. And You will come to me who asks. I am the Son You love. (Lesson 168)

♥ With eyes closed, follow your breath and focus on your Third Eye. To do this, look back at the point between your eyebrows, just below the center of your forehead. This posture stimulates the pineal gland.

Inbreath: As you inhale say the word "love" to yourself, feeling the Love of God filling you.

---

[54] Toning is informal chant, vocalizing a single tone at a comfortable pitch and holding it, using a vowel syllable such as "ah" or "ohm."

Outbreath: As you let your breath go say the word "God" to yourself, in trusting surrender to God, feeling the release and freedom of the "ah" sound.

Pause: Hold silence in the pause before the next inbreath.

As you breathe, notice the profound silence between each exhale and inhale. Notice how the silence is deeper between breaths. Delay the next inhale by a few seconds to expand this silence. When it feels right, shift your focus from the triad of breath, mantra and silence to the silence itself. Now everything takes a background to silence. Let the words "God" and "love" recede and keep focus on the silence between breaths. Watch the silence spread around you and "cover" the mantra of "love God." Carry the silence into each breath, cultivating the silence with your attention and making it the foreground.

♥ Imagine you are the point in the center of the infinite sphere of All That Is, at the cusp of space/time and eternity, simultaneously nothing and everything, always and only in the great circle of peace. Feel the peace. Be the peace.

♥ Focus on the idea *"I need do nothing."* Review the following, then sit in silence, feeling the expansive peace and freedom of having no tasks and no needs.

*To do anything involves the body. And if you recognize you need do nothing, you have withdrawn the body's value from your mind. Here is the quick and open door through which you slip past centuries of effort, and escape from time. This is the way in which sin [error] loses all attraction **right now**. For here is time denied, and past and future gone. Who needs do nothing has no need for time. To do nothing is to rest, and make a place within you where the activity of the body ceases to demand attention. Into this place the Holy Spirit comes, and there abides. He will remain when you forget, and the body's activities return to occupy your conscious mind.*

Yet there will always be this place of rest to which you can return. And you will be more aware of this quiet center of the storm than all its raging activity. This quiet center, in which you do nothing, will remain with you, giving you rest in the midst of every busy doing on which you are sent. For from this center will you be directed how to use the body sinlessly [without error]. It is this center, from which the body is absent, that will keep it so in your awareness of it.

(Text, Chapter 18:VII.7-8)

Vibrational Self-Healing

Toning with sacred syllables such as "aaaar-eeeeee-ohm" is an effective and beautiful way to begin and end meditation sessions, coaxing your whole being into resonance with the higher vibration you seek. To heal a broken heart, tone into the palm of each hand after meditating.

Hypno-Meditation

Hypno-meditation is silent meditation preceded by entering a state of hypnosis. It can be very helpful to beginning meditators and those of us who struggle with constant thinking and/or anxiety. Slowly read the following script into a recording device using a gentle, relaxed voice. Then simply play it back to yourself to begin each meditation session.

Script:[55] Put your back into a comfortable position it can stay in for a long time, separate your hands and uncross your legs. Take a deep breath in through the nose and let it out through the mouth. Close your eyes and allow yourself to imagine pure white light emanating from the highest source in the universe—bright, beautiful, pure light from the most peaceful, loving place. You know the source and can draw the light to you. . . . The light comes with the loving vibration of angelic music you have known forever. . . . Feel yourself gently wrapped in the velvet light. . . . Brilliant rainbows dance softly about. . . . The light is safe, and stands for everything good in life and beyond: peace— unconditional love—joy— abundance—healing—bliss—and complete relaxation. . . . Experiencing this pure light is your birthright, as you are *from* the light. . . . In truth you are one with the vibration of the light.

Allow the beautiful light to flow through every part of your being. As it flows from head to toe, let it completely relax each muscle. Feel the jaw relax and the lines of the forehead simply let go and spread apart. The light flows like a gentle waterfall through the facial muscles, down the neck and over the heart. . . also down the back of the head, neck and shoulders. Let gravity pull the shoulders down into their natural position. The body is at rest, and completely bathed in gently flowing, pure white light.

Notice the three parts to each breath. Breathing in there's a gentle expansion, then that pleasant sense of release as you exhale. And then a peaceful moment of stillness before you spontaneously inhale again, as you need it. Be aware of that peaceful pause. . . . Feel the pleasant, massage-like sensation to your breathing. The gentle stretching as you breathe in, the letting go as you breathe out, and that peaceful pause. . . . That feeling of letting go as you breathe out is exactly what relaxation feels like. . . .

Any thoughts just drift away. The mind is quiet and free. You'll still hear the relaxing sound of my voice, but it soon becomes just a comfortable feeling in the background. My words will blend and flow into your mind naturally, so you'll be free from having to *listen to* the words because the subconscious will recognize what they mean anyway. Words and thoughts just drift away like breath on a still winter evening.

[55] Portions of this script adapted from the work of Allen S. Chips, DCH, Ph.D., American Holistic University

Allow the pure white light to continue to bathe the body. Thoughts just drift away. Breathing becomes even deeper. With each relaxing breath, the mind quiets and the body rests more peacefully and deeply. As the light flows down the back, all the muscles let go and the back just settles into its best position. The light pours through the center of your being, bright and pure, down the spine, through the waist, knees, ankles, and out the toes. The body is awash in softly flowing, pure, white light. The light enfolds you in perfect peace.

. . . and now with each breath that you take, allow yourself to become more deeply relaxed—simply deeper with each breath. . . inhaling the light of peace and exhaling any thoughts or tension so that you may go deeper. . . deeper. . . and still deeper.

Imagine that you are floating toward your stillest, deepest level. You know where that level is, so you will simply feel yourself float there when I count from one to five. One, floating. Two, further. Three, more relaxed. Four, deeper. And five, deeply still and relaxed. . . .

When you have passed the amount of time you desire in the silence, you will awaken refreshed, alert, very satisfied, and feeling good. Decide now what time or in how many minutes you want to awaken. . . .

Now let go of all thoughts of the earth plane. Peace to your mind. . . . God is only Love, and therefore so are you. You are Love, and you enter the silence for remembering. As you take your place in the center of the great sphere of All That Is, the peace of God envelops you, and you forget all things except His Love. . . . Your thoughts are still. You rest in God: peace—love—safety—healing—joy—timelessness. You are spirit. You are *free*. This holy instant you give to God, receiving stillness and a tranquil, open mind. All the world departs in silence. You let illusions go quietly down to dust. . . and in this holy place of quiet you receive God's Word today.

Pain

Joy is just, and pain is but the sign you have misunderstood yourself. (Lesson 101)

Chrysoprase

Pain

Joy is just, and pain is but the sign you have misunderstood yourself. (Lesson 101)

Pain

All of Heaven's servants shower compassion on our pain, but these lovers of Love do not believe in it. We must learn not to believe in pain also. Instead we must learn to choose love now.

There are no scraps of dreams. Each one contains the whole of fear, the opposite of love, (in all its ways), the hell that hides the memory of God, the crucifixion of His holy Son. Therefore, be vigilant against them all, for in their single purpose they are one, and hell is total. It can seem to be forever for this lesson to be learned, and yet it need not be. I came to speak in time of timelessness. Have you not learned the pain of dreaming yet? . . .

The tiniest of dreams, the smallest wish for values of the world is large enough to stand between you and the sweet release that God would offer you. He cannot choose to change His Son, nor make your mind accept the perfect freedom He has given you . . . .

Everything the world can offer promises some joy that it will never give. And everything that God has promised you will never fail in anything. No need will be unmet, no hurt unhealed, no sorrow kept unchanged, no darkness undispelled. The smallest pain will vanish suddenly before His gifts.
(Urtext, G 1 A 6-7, *Volume VII, Gifts of God* [56], 1. *"The Dream of Fear"*)

When you are sad, KNOW that this NEED NOT BE. Depression ALWAYS arises ultimately from a sense of being deprived of something you want and do not have. Know you are deprived of nothing, except by your own decisions, and then decide otherwise.
(Urtext, T 4 E 6)

I felt betrayed and abandoned in my loss, very painful emotions. In the first several months, as I walked the path of this healing work, I cried frequently. I cried every day. I cried so reliably as I did my ACIM lessons that I put a box of tissues in my meditation area. Pain was often my companion, and my emotional state was almost comically schizophrenic, as I moved back and forth from pain to peace, despair to ecstasy. One moment I was Buddha—the next, a lost and frightened child bordering on hysteria. I understood that my pain must surface to be healed. It may inconvenience me and momentarily frighten me, but I remembered that pain is an opportunity for progress, as long as I work with it (instead of wallow in it), and as long as I ultimately remember that pain is not true. My Father, the God of Love, would never give me pain.

---

[56] The short work *Gifts of God* is dated 1978, after the first version of *A Course in Miracles* was published by the Foundation for Inner Peace in 1976.

Pain is a wrong perspective. . . . It is not a fact at all. There is no form it takes that will not disappear if seen aright. . . .

Pain is a sign illusions reign in place of truth. It demonstrates God is denied, confused with fear, perceived as mad, and seen as traitor to Himself. If God is real, there is no pain. If pain is real, there is no God. For vengeance is not part of love. And fear, denying love and using pain to prove that God is dead, has shown that death is victor over life. The body is the Son of God, corruptible in death, as mortal as the Father he has slain.

Peace to such foolishness! The time has come to laugh at such insane ideas. There is no need to think of them as savage crimes, or secret sins with weighty consequence. . . .

It is your thoughts alone that cause you pain. Nothing external to your mind can hurt or injure you in any way. There is no cause beyond yourself that can reach down and bring oppression. No one but yourself affects you. There is nothing in the world that has the power to make you ill or sad, or weak or frail. But it is you who have the power to dominate all things you see by merely recognizing what you are. As you perceive the harmlessness in them, they will accept your holy will as theirs. And what was seen as fearful now becomes a source of innocence and holiness.

My holy brother, think of this awhile: The world you see does nothing. It has no effects at all. It merely represents your thoughts. And it will change entirely as you elect to change your mind, and choose the joy of God as what you really want.

(Lesson 190)[57]

Ike – The world is what you think it is.

—Hawaiian Shamanic Principle[58]

---

[57] Integrating the truth of this passage from Lesson 190 to the extent that it manifests in every aspect of one's life is almost always a lengthy process. So please do not deny yourself treatment and comfort on the basis of the unreality of pain. When you are in pain, remind yourself that pain is NOT part of God's Reality and surrender it to God to be healed at the most basic level. Then speak with your counselor, consult with your doctor, follow your treatment plan, get a massage, take a pain killer, do your exercises, follow your diet, take your vitamins, do your emotional and mental healing work, adjust the ergonomics of your life, brush your teeth, get new shoes, etc., etc., etc. Freely do the "magic" things in the illusion that are recognized to be helpful for your pain, with gratitude and without guilt.

[58] as related by Serge Kahili King in *Urban Shaman*.

In the world we have "*special relationships*" that serve our ego purposes. Our "good" special relationships seem to provide us things we want, but believe we do not have. These are essentially the people and things we love, admire, and like. Our "bad" special relationships provide a screen on which to project what we have judged and rejected in ourselves. These would be our enemies, "difficult" people, and anyone or anything else we deem different in a negative way. Sometimes we have both special "good" and special "bad" relationships with the same person or thing.

But neither "good" nor "bad" special relationships truly serve to make us happy. Our special "good" relationships are monuments to separation, reinforcing the idea that we have lost our wholeness. "That which completes me is outside of me," would be an apt motto for special "good" relationships. Our special "bad" relationships are the very backbone of separation, continually providing "proof" that something or someone "out there" is the source of all problems.

A *holy relationship* is any special relationship that has been relinquished to the Holy Spirit for the purpose of mutual healing. Through holy relationships, the Holy Spirit dismantles the ego's purpose of maintaining separation and reinstates God's purpose of restoring the remembrance of Oneness. Forgiveness is the hallmark and language of a holy relationship.

Much of the pain of loss is about losing special "good" relationships. Let us retain our compassion for this pain, as everyone has felt it. Yet God calls to us to relinquish these relationships to the higher purposes of our healing. Through our losses we can reconnect to the One Source that authored our immutable wholeness. Let us open our hearts to consider the potential gift of healing that the loss of a loved one lays at our feet.[59]

The pain of loss, commonly known as grief, is rooted in our addiction to distraction. Grief is widely felt and, therefore, "normal" to us, but that does not change this underlying truth. Our *pain* is not about love and other lofty ideals. Love and empathy foster compassion, not grief. We are in pain or grieve because we became addicted, placing too much power in the person or thing that was lost. We used the lost person or thing to attempt to fill the God-shaped hole, the spiritual void in our being. When in pain we believe the departed person or thing defined and/or enhanced us in a way that is essential to our wholeness. We believe in our *need* so much that we feel pain when the person or thing is gone. We use any and all things to fill our emptiness and complete ourselves in this way—lovers, children, family, friends, pets, companionship, looks, health, jobs, careers, achievement, homes, money, possessions, activities, neighborhoods, nationalities, religions—everything.

---

[59] *We have said repeatedly that the Holy Spirit would not DEPRIVE you of your special relationships, but would TRANSFORM them. And by that, all that is meant is that He will RESTORE to them the function that was GIVEN them, by God. The function YOU have given them is clearly NOT to make happy. But the holy relationship SHARES God's purpose, rather than aiming to make a SUBSTITUTE for it. Every special relationship that YOU have made IS a substitute for God's Will, and glorifies yours instead of His, BECAUSE OF THE DELUSION THEY ARE DIFFERENT.*

You have VERY REAL relationships, even in this world, which you do not recognize, simply because you have raised their SUBSTITUTES to such predominance that, when truth calls to you, as it does constantly, YOU ANSWER WITH A SUBSTITUTE. Every special relationship which you have ever undertaken has, as its fundamental purpose, the aim of occupying your minds so completely that YOU WILL NOT HEAR the call of truth. In a sense, the special relationship was the EGO'S answer to the creation of the Holy Spirit, Who was God's answer to the separation. For, although the ego did not understand WHAT had been created, it WAS aware of threat. (Urtext, T 17 E 2-3)

We may feel that "addiction" is too harsh a concept or not always applicable—what about the grief of a mother who loses a child whom she loved purely and unconditionally? Or the grief over a suicide or murder? How about the grief over an accidental or untimely death? Or the grief over another's pain or illness or abuse?

There is no error in compassion—a loving preference that others not suffer. The error is in addiction to the illusion of the status quo, and the pain that results from that addiction.

Even though nothing in this world is permanent, life is not a series of losses. It is a journey of "groops," "foops," and "loops"—growth opportunities, forgiveness opportunities, and love opportunities—all one and the same. *Opportunity* is what painful experiences are for.

We may judge that God is ineffective, apathetic, or vindictive when events happen that we don't readily comprehend. How can a loving God work through suffering and death for our good? The answer is that God is eternal, omnipresent, all-loving, all-powerful, and all-knowing. God works through all ego decisions for the collective good, transmuting darkness to light. No one exits a bus, much less the earth plane, without God maximizing the potential benefit to all throughout time. This includes the deceased and survivors, victims and perpetrators, the joyous and the tortured. Since death is not real, there is no *real* reason to be upset.

For death is not OF the real world, in which everything is eternal. (Urtext, T 11 D 9)

I do not perceive my own best interests. (Lesson 24)

My sadness is about how the absence of my loved one affects me and my life. If I believe in the eternal God of Love, how can I be sad that my loved one has passed out of this realm where "God is not," presumably further along the way of remembering Oneness with Him?

My upset shows that I believe more in bodies than spirit. If I believe in our identity as the spirit children of Love, how can I be upset about the death of any mere body, including my own?

My condemnation of a loss reveals my unwillingness to accept responsibility or my lack of trust. If I believe that I have invented the world I see and that God works through all things for the good and healing of all, how can I condemn any particular event?

My judgment is simply the cover for my projections, which in turn cover my sense of guilt and fear. If I believe that I *"cannot but be in the right place at the right time,"*[60] how can any event be "wrong"?

I am God's Son, complete and healed and whole, shining in the reflection of His Love. In me is His creation sanctified and guaranteed eternal life. In me is love perfected, fear impossible, and joy established without opposite. I am the holy home of God Himself. I am the Heaven where His Love resides. I am His holy Sinlessness Itself, for in my purity abides His Own.

---

[60] *God is indeed your strength, and what He gives is truly given. This means that you can receive it any time and anywhere, wherever you are and in whatever circumstances you find yourself. Your passage through time and space is not random. You cannot but be in the right place at the right time. Such is the strength of God. Such are His gifts.* (Lesson 42)

. . . we can realize our function here, and words can speak of this and teach it, too, if we exemplify the words in us.

We are the bringers of salvation. We accept our part as saviors of the world, which through our joint forgiveness is redeemed. . . . We look on everyone as brother, and perceive all things as kindly and as good. . . . We are concerned only with giving welcome to the truth. . . .

And from the oneness that we have attained we call to all our brothers, asking them to share our peace and consummate our joy.

We are the holy messengers of God who speak for Him, and carrying His Word to everyone whom He has sent to us, we learn that it is written on our hearts. And thus our minds are changed about the aim for which we came, and which we seek to serve. We bring glad tidings to the Son of God, who thought he suffered. Now is he redeemed. And as he sees the gate of Heaven stand open before him, he will enter in and disappear into the Heart of God.

(Workbook, Part II, 14. *"What am I?"*)

If I am upset over death, it is either because I doubt God's Reality (believing instead in the body's seeming reality) or because I value the illusion of the world more. When I value worldly things (including special people), I am ultimately concerned with how they affect me. Look at how personal motives and delusions underlie these "selfless" expressions of grief:

He died before his time and won't be able to experience life and love.
- I and/or others won't be able to experience life with him, so life will be meaningless or sad.
- Now I can't love him, and I can't feel his love for me.
- I want/deserve the life I planned for myself, not the purpose God plans for me.
- If he is vulnerable, I am vulnerable. I have reason to fear.
- Life on Earth IS as I perceive it, and I say it's tragic if a life gets cut short in my estimation.

She was murdered—it isn't right!
- I understand the big picture enough to judge it.
- If she is vulnerable, I am vulnerable. I have reason to fear.
- Life on Earth IS as I perceive it, and I say murder is unforgiveable.

Is it possible that a murder is a lesson chosen, a result cultivated, or karmic balancing? Perhaps the "victim" is helping the perpetrator to complete an essential lesson. Perhaps the "perpetrator" is helping the victim, survivors, and/or society to complete essential lessons.

She was sick and in pain—it isn't fair!

- I can be punished by God, but when I make the body real God is no longer in charge. I am now in charge, because I am the author of death.
- I understand the big picture enough to judge it.
- If she is vulnerable, I am vulnerable. I have reason to fear.
- Life on Earth IS as I perceive it, and I say I can suffer and die.

Is it possible that illness is a lesson chosen, a result cultivated, or karmic balancing? Perhaps the "victim" is helping herself or others (loved ones, caregivers) to complete essential lessons.

He died for no reason (accident or illness).
- I understand the big picture enough to judge it.
- If he is vulnerable, I am vulnerable. I have reason to fear.
- Life on Earth IS as I perceive it, and I say it is random. God is not in charge.

I am so devastated that she killed herself.
- I didn't love her enough to save her.
- She didn't love me enough to stay.

I feel so sorry for her family and friends.
- I am guilty. My pain will somehow atone for the pain of others.
- If they are vulnerable, I am vulnerable. I have reason to fear.

Of course it's not "wrong" or "bad" to feel pain. But healing requires that I see it clearly. Pain is simply the end result of the erroneous ego thought system. The belief in sin, guilt, and fear makes a *solution* of victimhood—the idea that you (outside of me) are the cause of what I feel and do—that *your* action or inaction, presence or absence, approval or disapproval, or ebb or flow affects *my* peace. Victimhood is the ego's solution to the supposed wrath of God because victimhood makes me feel and appear less guilty than you, and therefore less vulnerable. Rather than remaining a victim, *accepting and defending pain* as a part of love, I am called to *transcend* my small self and the ego thought system that breeds pain. I am called to recognize my immutable oneness and safety by resting in the Truth of Love—my real nature, or Self.

> *Love is the Law of God. You live that you may learn to love. You love that you may learn to live. No other lesson is required of Man. And what is it to love but for the lover to absorb forever the beloved so that the twain be one? . . . No love is possible except the love of self. No self is real save the All-embracing Self. Therefore is God all Love, because He loves Himself. So long as you are pained by Love, you have not found your real self, nor have you found the golden key of Love. Because you love an ephemeral self, your love is ephemeral.*
>
> *(The Book of Mirdad)*[61]

---

[61] Mikhail Naimy

Addiction cannot be quelled with more of the craved substance. That "solution" is a never-ending spiral into oblivion fueled by the mirage of more. The answer to addiction (the belief that we need something outside of ourselves) is the knowledge—gained through experience—that we are inherently whole, whole without anything outside ourselves—whole because God, our Father, is found within us. When we embrace God wholly, we remember we are holy.

> *Eternal holiness abides in me.*
> *Only an instant does this world endure.* (Lessons 299, 300)

Walking the path of pain in healing, we must remember the painful truth: pain is not the sign of truth. Peace is the sign of truth. Emotional pain, just like physical pain, is a signal that something needs to be healed.

> *Truth will correct all errors in my mind.*
> *I am mistaken when I think I can be hurt in any way.*
> *I am God's Son, whose Self rests safely in the Mind of God.* (Lesson 119)

When you feel pain over and over about the same thing, it's not because that thing is real and powerful. For example, missing someone is not proof that you truly love that person; it's proof that you have an emptiness you have been using him or her to fill. Pain is repetitious because its cause remains unhealed. That is all. It's just the snooze alarm ringing again, until, through healing, you wake up and silence the alarm once and for all.

> *I choose the joy of God instead of pain.* (Lesson 190)

> *. . . Lay down your arms, and come without defense into the quiet place where Heaven's peace holds all things still at last. . . . Here you will understand there is no pain. . . . [Now] it is given you to realize the lesson that contains all of salvation's power. It is this: Pain is illusion; joy, reality. Pain is but sleep; joy is awakening. Pain is deception; joy alone is truth.*

> *And so again we make the only choice that ever can be made; we choose between illusions and the truth, or pain and joy, or hell and Heaven. Let our gratitude unto our Teacher fill our hearts, as we are free to choose our joy instead of pain, our holiness in place of sin, the peace of God instead of conflict, and the light of Heaven for the darkness of the world.* (Lesson 190)

In this world of illusion, even the most painstaking "truth" down to the most minute detail isn't True. All the facts of that which never happened will only add up to falsehood. Love Is, and so pain simply cannot be true.

Pain released and replaced with the fruits of forgiveness—peace, love, joy, abundance, and safety—is magnificent progress. This is the work in life that is worth doing.

Pain resisted is pain multiplied. Learn to relax and accept each moment as it is and as it comes.

Let all things be exactly as they are. (Lesson 268)

Let not our sight be blasphemous today, nor let our ears attend to lying tongues. Only reality is free of pain. Only reality is free of loss. Only reality is wholly safe. And it is only this we seek today. (Lesson 268)

We side with truth and let illusions go. We will not vacillate between the two, but take a firm position with the One. We dedicate ourselves to truth today, and to salvation as God planned it be. We will not argue it is something else, we will not seek for it where it is not. In gladness we accept it as it is, and take the part assigned to us by God. (Lesson 98)

Although it may feel discouraging to *feel* so much pain as you heal, bear in mind two things:

1. There is no way around pain but through it.

2. In Truth we are One. Therefore, every ounce of healing you accomplish personally is a gift to all the children of God, as well as yourself. Your healing is service, so hang in there![62]

When I am healed, I am not healed alone. (Lesson 137)

Salvation of the world depends on me. (Lesson 186)

Pain results from fear. This correlation is easy to see in the pain of loss, where, for example, the pain may be about such fears as never finding equal happiness again, being unworthy or unlovable, not knowing what to do next, or that the future will continue to be sad.

Fear is not justified in any form. Not one thing in this world is true. (Lesson 240)

What could you not accept, if you but knew that everything that happens, all events, past, present and to come, are gently planned by One Whose only purpose is your good? Perhaps you have misunderstood His plan, for He would never offer pain to you. (Lesson 135)

---

[62] *And as you let yourself be healed, you see all those around you, or who cross your mind, or whom you touch, or those who seem to have no contact with you, healed along with you. Perhaps you will not recognize them all, nor realize how great your offering to all the world, when you let healing come to you. But you are never healed alone. And legions upon legions will receive the gift which you receive when you are healed.*

Those who are healed become the instruments of healing. Nor does time elapse between the instant they are healed and all the grace of healing it is given them to give. What is opposed to God does not exist, and who accepts it not within his mind becomes a haven where the weary can remain to rest. For here is truth bestowed, and here are all illusions brought to truth. (Lesson 137)

If God would not offer pain to me, there must be another way to see the things I perceive as painful. Pain, like everything else on the earth plane, is really a matter of perception. Knowing that perception is changeable, and therefore not truth, reveals that pain is a matter of choice—a choice involving false perception.

Whatever suffers is not part of me. (Lesson 248)

I have disowned the truth. Now let me be as faithful in disowning falsity. Whatever suffers is not part of me. What grieves is not myself. What is in pain is but illusion in my mind. What dies was never living in reality, and did but mock the truth about myself. Now I disown self-concepts and deceits and lies about the holy Son of God. Now am I ready to accept him back as God created him, and as he is. (Lesson 248)

The Course makes clear that the solution to pain is forgiveness. Pray daily to master the habit of forgiveness. For example:

Father, I am willing to forgive anything that comes into my awareness without exception and without reserve. Let me perceive forgiveness as it is. I forgive illusions, not truth. I will forgive, and my pain will disappear because forgiveness ends all suffering and loss.[63]

Have you ever felt forgiveness stinks? It's just the smell of karma burning.

As we do our emotional and mental healing work, our pain and anger will be released, more of our true identity will be revealed, and the promises of peace and joy will come true.

My present happiness is all I see. (Lesson 290)
I can be free of suffering today. (Lesson 340)
I will receive whatever I request. I want the peace of God. (Lessons 339, 185)

In Rick Ray's film, *10 Questions for the Dalai Lama*, His Holiness the 14th Dalai Lama of Tibet was asked how Buddhism can have an impact on the conflict between warring religions in the Middle East. Recognizing the efforts of individuals toward peace, harmony, and open-mindedness His Holiness replied, "All major world religious traditions have the same potential to create harmony, to create peace of mind. Too much emotion—negative emotion—frustrations, hatred, anger—that's the greatest obstacle. This should be cooled down— reduced. Forget these things—for the time being have more festivals, make personal friends. Then talk about these serious matters." I believe the Dalai Lama means we are to distance ourselves from pain and cultivate joy in our lives, interact personally with others, and love them—love people over ideologies. Loving people involves the liberal practice of forgiveness.

---

[63] Adapted from the Introduction to Lesson 300, and Lessons 134 and 249

Grieve Not As Others Grieve

If you are feeling pain over the loss of someone who has passed over, it is especially important to walk through your pain into healing. Not only is this the route you must take to move forward in your own life, *your* pain and grief also impede the soul of your loved one in its task of letting go of the earth plane and moving on. Your prolonged grief becomes shackles to both of you, not an expression of love.

The Course counsels us to forgive and *"God Himself shall wipe away all tears."*[64] I am not suggesting that mourning be bypassed. I am reminding us to employ our mourning for healing. Many cultures developed a timed ritual for mourning, which implies two things. There is a time to express our grief, and a time to set it aside and get back to life. Of course we should honor our human grief by allowing space and time to express our authentic emotions and sit with our emptiness and disorientation. This emotional purging is part of the healing process. And if we have unresolved issues with the departed, we also address these in our emotional and mental healing work. Having done this, we then call upon concentration and willpower—our ability to focus and control our own thinking—and lovingly move on, cherishing in our hearts the love we shared, but not clinging addictively to the memory of our loved one.

---

[64] (Lesson 301)

Anger and Forgiveness

Let me remember I am one with God, at one with all my brothers and my Self,
in everlasting holiness and peace. (Lesson 124)

Kunzite

Anger and Forgiveness

*Let me remember I am one with God, at one with all my brothers and my Self,
in everlasting holiness and peace.* (Lesson 124)

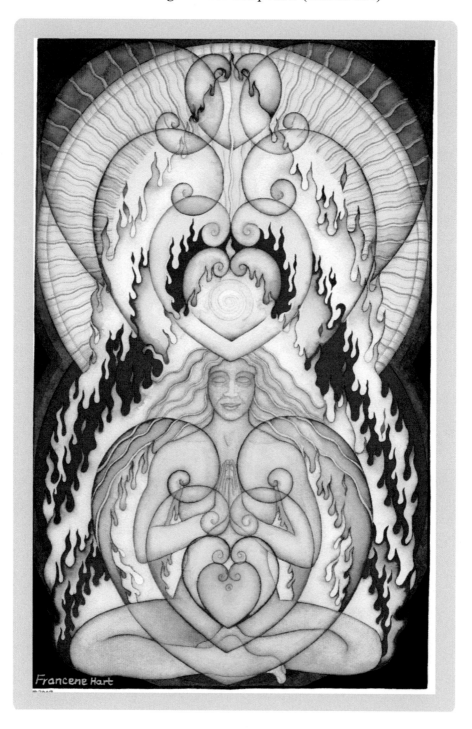

Anger and Forgiveness

"I am God's Son, complete and healed and whole, shining in the reflection of His Love."[65]

Until you "piss me off." This is a joke, of course! You can't "piss me off." I can't "piss you off." Each of us has full responsibility for our perceptions of and reactions to people, events, and things in our world.

> *I am not the victim of the world I see.*
> *I have invented the world I see.*
> *Forgiveness is the key to happiness.* (Lessons 31, 32, 121)

Forgiveness is commonly known as the "healthy" and "spiritual" way to deal with anger and disappointment in others by letting go of our reaction to some event. But this view is incomplete.

A Technical Definition of Forgiveness: Complete forgiveness is reclaiming my spiritual identity of innocence and wholeness through the process of transmuting projection (based on separation and judgment) into compassion and love. The way is through oneness—recognizing my connection with all things that I formerly perceived as less than or greater than myself—things I perceived as disturbing or attractive.

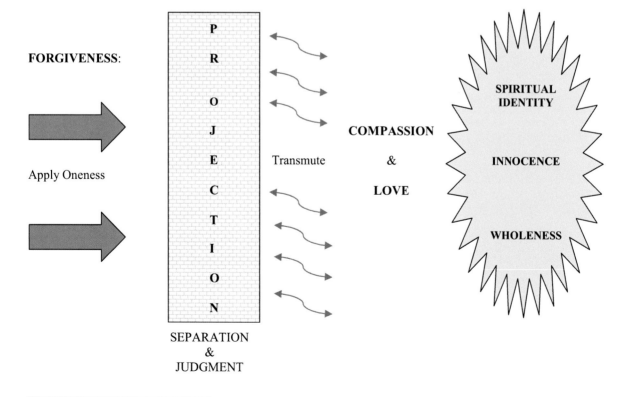

FORGIVENESS:

Apply Oneness

P R O J E C T I O N

SEPARATION & JUDGMENT

Transmute

COMPASSION & LOVE

SPIRITUAL IDENTITY

INNOCENCE

WHOLENESS

---

[65] (Workbook, Part II, 14. *"What am I?"*)

Forgiveness tears down the wall of projection built on separation and judgment. By applying oneness we transmute projection to compassion and love, in which we recover our true spiritual identity of innocence and wholeness.

Forgiveness is like the sea rolling onto a beach, erasing the footprints of all who walked there and leaving the sand pristine, shaped only by the singular force of the ocean. Forgiveness washes away the debris of separation, judgment, and projection from our lives, allowing the energy of love to dominate and shape our experience. Forgiveness purifies all and allows us to choose love now.

> *Forgiveness recognizes what you thought your brother did to you has not occurred. It does not pardon sins and make them real. It sees there was no sin. And in that view are all your sins forgiven.*
> (Workbook, Part II, 1. *"What Is Forgiveness?"*)

The things we come to forgive—our forgiveness opportunities—are not real because they are constructed from our projections. In anger we walk into a brightly lit room wearing dark sunglasses and complain about the lack of light. The darkness we perceive isn't real, it's just the result of the filters over our eyes—our projections.

If grappling with anger counts, I am an expert. I have been an adept channel of the bitch archetype. I first became aware that I was angry at age 22 during treatment for major depression. At that time in my life, I sometimes felt so angry I would literally see stars. Then, when I got sober, another avalanche of anger flooded my consciousness. Anger has been my number one challenge ever since this first awareness, although I am grateful that anger is much less prevalent in my mind, words, and actions than it used to be. My anger has prompted me to learn what anger really is and many ways to dismantle it.

The presence of anger may not be obvious when you are feeling grief, but it is probably there.[66] Anger is a defense against painful emotions, an attempt at relief through projection onto someone or something else. Some of the pain felt in grief is likely to be expressed as anger. The Course makes clear that the intensity of anger does not matter.

> *. . . anger may take the form of any reaction ranging from mild irritation to rage. The degree of the emotion you experience does not matter. . . a slight twinge of annoyance is nothing but a veil drawn over intense fury.* (Lesson 21)

Again, whether you would rate your feeling as irritation, annoyance, frustration, anger, fury, rage, or any nuance in between or beyond is irrelevant.

> [regarding slight irritation or intense rage]. . . *It does not matter. All of these reactions are the same. They obscure the truth, and this can never be a matter of degree. Either truth is apparent, or it is not. It cannot be partially recognized. Who is unaware of truth must look upon illusions.*
> (Manual for Teachers, 17. *"How Do God's Teachers Deal with Magic Thoughts?"*)

---

[66] Elisabeth Kübler-Ross identified anger as the second among the five stages of grief in her classic work, *On Death and Dying*.

What goes around comes around—for forgiveness.

In healing loss (or anything else), anger must be handled responsibly through forgiveness. This need for forgiveness applies both to the anger you feel and may express and the anger that may be expressed to you. Anger is a toxic spill that mires whoever believes in it in the illusion of separation and "not God." The goal is to "over-look" (look beyond) errors such as anger and the conditions that seem to be their source. To accomplish this we must use the spiritual eye. We must raise our eyes to look *over* the dense judgments of the world and focus on higher truths.

> *To study the error itself does not lead to correction, if you are indeed to succeed in overlooking the error. And it is just this process of overlooking at which the course aims.* (Manual for Teachers, Clarification of Terms, *Introduction*)

Our true identity as the Son of God is unassailable and needs no defense. Therefore anger is not necessary.

> *I am mistaken when I think I can be hurt in any way.*
> *I am God's Son, whose Self rests safely in the Mind of God.* (Lesson 119)

We have been receiving spiritual messages about transcending anger for a long time:

> *Thou preparest a table before me in the presence of mine enemies:*
> *thou anointest my head with oil; my cup runneth over.* (Psalm 23:5)

When I let go of my anger and forgive those who seem to have hurt me, I receive the Blessing of God and radiate love without limit.

> *Ye have heard that it hath been said, An eye for an eye, and a tooth for a tooth:*
> *But I say unto you, That ye resist not evil: but whosoever shall smite thee on thy*
> *right cheek, turn to him the other also.* (Matthew 5:38-39)

Do not attack in response to perceived attack. Stay in defenselessness.

> *But I say unto you which hear, Love your enemies, do good to them which hate you,*
> *Bless them that curse you, and pray for them which despitefully use you.*
> *And unto him that smiteth thee on the one cheek offer also the other;*
> *and him that taketh away thy cloak forbid not to take thy coat also.*
> *Give to every man that asketh of thee;*
> *and of him that taketh away thy goods ask them not again.*
> *And as ye would that men should do to you, do ye also to them likewise.*
> (Luke 6:27-31)

Do not retaliate for perceived attack and love your brother with gentleness, *as yourself.*

Practice the science of I-don't-mind.—Swami Beyondananda

With a spiritual solution properly applied, anger becomes a stepping stone, a means to elevate our consciousness. In other words, anger can function as a blessing, but ONLY when we do the work to leave it behind.

> *Turning the other cheek does NOT mean that you should submit to violence without protest. It means that you cannot be hurt, and do not want to show your brother anything except your wholeness. Show him that he CANNOT hurt you, and hold nothing against him, or you hold it against yourself.* (Urtext, 5 F 11)

We are not asked to be doormats. We must take care of ourselves, but not in anger. When we are wronged, we accept what is happening and then may choose to say something or do something (such as pursue an equitable solution, a lawsuit, an arrest, or simply leave) and then gather our whole, unharmed selves and continue on with our lives. We are called to *over-look* (look beyond), not ignore, abuse. When we do not take care of ourselves, we aid and abet the choice of another to engage in abusive behavior, to the spiritual detriment of both of us. In such a case, *neither* person's behavior is a loving reflection of the Son of God.

If you are irritated by every rub, how will you be polished?—Rumi

It should be emphasized that the most advanced response is a quiet acceptance of what is— that someone is calling out for love in an unloving way—without a punitive reaction to the notion that we have been hurt and trying to get the world to agree with us. This may mean letting (meaningless) material objects and worldly concepts go, but it does not mean a child of God must submit to abuse:

> *Resistance is the sire of anger; there is no mercy and no reason in a wrathful man. I tell you it is better far to suffer loss than go to law, or call upon the courts of men to judge of right and wrong.*
>
> *The law of carnal man would say, Eye for eye and tooth for tooth; resist encroachment on your rights. But this is not the law of God. The Holy Breath would say, Resist not him who would deprive you of your goods. He who would take your coat by force is still a brother man and you should gain his heart, which by resistance cannot be done. Give him your coat and offer him still more and more; in time the man will rise above the brute; you will have saved him from himself.*
>
> *. . . Be merciful unto your foes; bless those who slander you; do good to those who do you harm and pray for those who trample on your rights.*
>
> *Remember, you are children of the God who makes his sun to rise alike upon the evil and the good, who sends his rain upon the unjust and the just.*

If you do unto other men as they do unto you, you are but slaves, but followers in the way to death. But you, as children of the light, must lead the way. Do unto others as you would have them do unto you.
(*The Aquarian Gospel of Jesus the Christ*, Section XVI, Chapter 97:14-19, 25-29)

Here on Earth we are one in our innate goodness as well as the illusion of separation.

This is the first lesson ye should learn: There is so much good in the worst of us, and so much bad in the best of us, it doesn't behoove any of us to speak [or believe] evil of the rest of us. This is a universal law, and until one begins to make application of same, one may not go very far in spiritual or soul development.
(Edgar Cayce Reading 3063-1)

The Course clearly states that the multitude of problems we seem to suffer on Earth stem from one and only one core problem: the (insane) belief that we are separate from God. The way, then, to solve all problems is to solve this one. The solution is forgiveness.[67] The result is recovering our awareness of being one with God—a state in which problems are impossible.

Let not my world obscure the sight of Christ. . . . Perception is a mirror, not a fact. And what I look on is my state of mind, reflected outward. I would bless the world by looking on it through the eyes of Christ. (Lesson 304)

Forgiveness (seeing without judgment "through the eyes of Christ") is the single answer to all suffering.

Only my condemnation injures me. Only my own forgiveness sets me free. . . .
Do not forget . . . that there can be no form of suffering that fails to hide an unforgiving thought.
Nor can there be a form of pain forgiveness cannot heal. (Lesson 198)

Forgiveness is the answer to all pain, and lurking within all pain must be some unforgiveness, or fear. Anger is a defense against fear, an attempt to get rid of vulnerability. We are afraid that the future will turn out like the past, that we will be hurt yet again. Our fear makes us prisoners to the past.

Condemn and we are made prisoners. Forgive and we are set free.—Jon Mundy

Forgiveness is the answer to anger and all other judgment because of the Law of Love:

---

[67] [The Holy Spirit] *must use EVERYTHING in this world for your release. He must side with EVERY sign or token of your willingness to learn of Him what truth MUST be. He is swift to utilize WHATEVER you offer Him, on behalf of this. His concern and care for you are limitless. In the face of your fear of forgiveness, which He perceives as clearly as He knows forgiveness IS release, He will teach you to remember always that forgiveness is NOT loss, BUT YOUR SALVATION. And that, in COMPLETE forgiveness, in which you recognize that there is nothing to forgive, YOU are absolved completely.* (Urtext, T 15 I 2)

To give and receive are one in truth. (Lesson 108)

The practice of forgiveness is allowing others to show you where you have failed to forgive yourself, and then forgiving both of you.

All that I give is given to myself. (Lesson 126)

When I over-look your seeming error, I open my spiritual eye that can grasp your innocence. Only when I perceive your innocence do I also perceive my own. Projection, which promises to prove my innocence by moving my guilt outward onto others, is only a *reaction* to my own guilt. Projection thus "verifies" my guilt and locks me into the bondage of resentment (because I continue to believe I have been hurt) and further guilt (because I feel guilty for projecting my guilt onto others). But forgiveness restores innocence to both the receiver and the giver, and thus sets me free.

> *Anger is NEVER justified. Attack has NO foundation. . . . Pardon is ALWAYS justified. It has a sure foundation. You do NOT forgive the unforgivable, nor overlook a REAL attack that calls for punishment.* (Urtext, 30 G 1)

Owning and retrieving our projections is not only the mechanism of true forgiveness, it is also the "secret ingredient" that distinguishes compassion from pity. Compassion feels good because it is an energy of unity and love. Pity feels horrendous because it is an energy of separation and the ego.

Forgiveness is unraveling the threads of tangled illusions back to the simple truth that God Is.

Content vs. Form

The concept of "content vs. form" is useful in understanding the workings of forgiveness. To effectively forgive, we focus on *content* (the big, spiritual picture) over *form* (the individual, worldly details). As Byron Katie says about her process of inquiry called The Work, "we are working on concepts [content], not people [form]." Dealing with *content* is sure and efficient because we address cause, rather than effect, thus ensuring an effect in our lives. But we access our *content*, our core issues, through the *form* or details of our lives. Dealing *only* with form keeps us scattered, confused, and exhausted as we flit from one problem to the next, trying to put out one fire while sparking another—never dealing with cause at all. On the other hand, dealing with *content through form* is an exquisite gift of efficiency from our Father via the Holy Spirit.

Forgiveness recognizes that others are not guilty because their "offenses" are an illusion of projection. Nothing has truly occurred. Practicing forgiveness at this level of non-duality, I heal the core issues of my soul (*content*) through the easily reached details of my everyday life (*form*). This most profound spiritual practice is always at my fingertips in the mundane occurrences of my daily life.

In the grief of loss, seeing our own anger may sometimes be a stretch. Where is the anger, or unforgiving thought, when we just feel heartbroken over a loss? Here are some ideas to ponder:

Under the surface of my pain and grief I believe:

> I deserve to be or must be _____ (happy, fulfilled, successful, comfortable, etc.) *and that means* _____ (being with a particular person, having my possessions, living in this house, etc.), and now that has been taken away from me. Therefore I have been attacked, and I'm angry about it.

Entitlement underlies anger. As the Son of God, I *am* entitled to miracles—a new way of seeing through the eyes of love. I am a creator and manifestor. But I am not *entitled* to having my way in the world. I am entitled to choosing peace at any time.

The best defense is a sneak offense.—the Ego

Under the surface of my pain and grief I believe:

> Without _____, (person, job, possession, health, quality) I am not safe. I am vulnerable. If I am vulnerable, that means something from outside can attack me—which makes me angry. If I can be attacked, I must attack in self-defense.

Indeed we do believe we are vulnerable because of our own anger. If I can judge you, hurt you, project my guilt onto you, and make you more guilty than me (and in the illusion I believe that I can do all of these), then I am vulnerable to the same from you. Every idea of anger I have weakens me. The more I try to project it onto you, the weaker I feel. The weaker I feel, the more I feel attacked and respond with anger. This sad illusion cycles round and round in our lives with no hope for ending, *but* through forgiveness.

Anger must come from judgment.
Judgment is the weapon I would use against myself,
to keep the miracle away from me. (Lesson 347)

I can stop the cycle of anger and vulnerability only by practicing forgiveness. I must remember to recognize the truth that, as spirit conceived and held eternally within Love, only seeming caught in an illusory world, injury is not possible. I can neither deal effective blows nor receive them. This world can touch me not. The prince of this world comes and finds nothing in me.[68] I simply let go of what has no meaning in truth and choose love now. I focus on God's Truth—the reality of peace, love, joy, abundance, and safety—and I am rich.

Forgiveness is the revenge of the rich.

For some, including myself, forgiveness is much more easily understood in theory than practiced in the heat of the moment. Nonetheless, forgiveness IS the answer, so we practice until it is

---

[68] *Hereafter I will not talk much with you: for the prince of this world cometh, and hath nothing in me.* (Matthew 14:30)

mastered. Like researchers of the heart, we survey the literature and experiment to find the methods that work for us.

Forgiveness is the science of the heart: a discipline of discovering all the ways of being that will extend your love to the world, and discarding all the ways that do not.   —D. Patrick Miller

And like shaman, we already know the answer.

Kala – There are no limits. There are no limits to my forgiveness.
—Hawaiian Shamanic Principle[69]

---

[69] as related by Serge Kahili King in *Urban Shaman.*

Subject Projection Infections to New Direction

Nine Methods for Dispelling Anger

You do not have to remain bewitched by the spell of anger. To stop your anger (or another emotion) in its tracks, turn and observe the anger with your "witness consciousness." This does not mean observing your behavior, or sympathizing with or entertaining thoughts about your anger, or attempting to control it. Just give it your attention. Look at your anger and it will melt away because now you have identified with the calm, accepting observer in you (the witness), instead of the ego that is having the emotional experience. This kind of observation will release you from feeling an emotion, but you still have the effects in your body and the cause—your thoughts—to deal with.

Ask God for help in one or more ways. The Course offers many tools for this (1-6), there is a popular solution from the Bible (7), one from Michael Mirdad (8), and one I adapted from *The Way of Mastery* (9):

1. Help me see this brother through the eyes of truth, and not of judgment. Help me see this brother with "Christ's vision."[70]

2. insert name, *"I give you to the Holy Spirit as part of myself. I know you will be released unless I want to use you to imprison myself. In the name of my freedom I choose your release, because I recognize that we will be released together."*
(Text, Chapter 15:XI.10)

3. Ask God to purify your thoughts of your judgments. (Lesson 151)[71]

4. Ask and affirm, *"Give me your blessing, Holy Son of God."* (Lesson 161)

5. Refuse to entertain angry thoughts. Ask instead, *"Would I condemn myself for doing this?"* Affirm your choice not to run your grievance in your head. *"I rule my mind, which I alone must rule."* (Lessons 134, 236)[72]

6. Seek further refuge from your (insane) lapse into anger in meditation.

---

[70] (Lessons 158, 159, 161, 162, 164)

[71] *Your ministry begins as all your thoughts are purified.* (Lesson 151:15.2)

[72] *Let me perceive forgiveness as it is.* (Lesson 134) We don't forgive *anything* that is real. There is nothing to forgive in that which is real, as it is unified, wholly of God. What we forgive is always illusion—illusion that merely seems real in our experience. The lesson suggests that for every event or thing that comes to mind to forgive, we ask "Would I CONDEMN myself for doing this?" That is much different from the question, "Would I do this?" which feels so easy to deny when we are projecting and angry.

7. Pray with sincerity and enthusiasm for the peace, happiness, and prosperity of the one with whom you are feeling angry. *"Bless those who curse you, pray for those who abuse you."* (Luke 6:28)

8. Do *Michael Mirdad's Healing/Forgiveness Process* on the situation. Track underneath your anger to the deeper, core issue. (This process is covered in the chapter "Emotional Healing Work.")

9. Do the *Mastery Forgiveness Process*, covered later in this chapter.

Note that none of these forgiveness methods call for telling another person you have forgiven him. Announcing *your* forgiveness of another is a way of passing judgment, and in effect reinforces the idea that he has hurt you. Forgiveness is internal work with both internal and external effects. The results of forgiveness will manifest naturally. It is often unnecessary to say "I forgive you," unless you are asked. Let the Holy Spirit guide you in the most loving course of action.

> *EXTENSION of forgiveness is the Holy Spirit's function. Leave this to Him. Let YOUR concern be only that you give TO Him that which can BE extended. Save no dark secrets that He cannot use. But offer Him the tiny gifts He can extend forever.*
> (Urtext, T 22 G 9)

In addition to applying spiritual principles to your anger, discharge anger and other negative emotions from the body with responsible physical activity. This physical activity can include, for example, walking, running, and other forms of exercise; hitting balls and other sports; pounding or screaming into pillows; bodywork; and bioenergetics. Discharging anger must substantially engage the physical body (target shooting, video games and chess, for example, do NOT have enough bodily movement) and be safe—hurting no one, including yourself.

Forgiveness takes the wind out of the sails of your warship.

Gratitude

We will learn to cultivate gratitude toward those who inspire our anger, because in truth they are showing us the way home. They are "teaching" us by providing an opportunity to learn our crucial lessons of forgiveness, thereby acting as steps on the stairway to Heaven.

You see his madness, which you hate because you SHARE in it.[73]

---

[73] *To look upon the fear of God DOES need some preparation. Only the sane can look on stark insanity and raving madness with pity and compassion, but NOT with fear. For only if you SHARE in it does it seem fearful, and you DO share in it until you look upon each other with perfect faith and love and tenderness. Before complete forgiveness, you still stand unforgiving. You are afraid of God BECAUSE you fear each other. Those you do not forgive, YOU FEAR. And no-one reaches love, with FEAR beside him.*

This brother, who stands beside you, still seems to be a stranger. You do NOT know him, and your INTERPRE-

And so we practice by silently saying:

Give me your blessing, holy Son of God. (Lesson 161)

Applied to *anyone* who tempts you to anger or fear, this idea of receiving a blessing from the "cause" of your negative reaction is your safe escape. Instead of holding onto your anger with someone, for example, remember that whatever you find objectionable in him is only a manifestation of some wound of your own. Instead of dwelling on this illusion, choose to see the other as part of your mind, part of the One Mind, rejected from yourself and projected outward. Identify the energy of the situation that is upsetting or triggering you. Then consider when you have related with the same energy to another. This focus on *energy* releases you from the worldly particulars, those details which might "prove" that you have NEVER done such a thing. When you realize you have shared the energy behind an act, then you can see yourself and the other with compassion—not as *bodies* and *guilty*, but as the Christ, God's perfect Son. And thus you perceive the truth of your own sinlessness, the blessing of all blessings in this world.

I'm OKAY, you're. . . hmmm. . . (practicing forgiveness). . . okay. . . I really *am* okay!

If you are only love, therefore so am I. I am only love and, therefore, so are you. In thought and action, practice taking back your projections of guilt. Don't expect perfection, but "fake it 'til you make it," and you will someday come to feel gratitude for the "difficult" people in your life, just as many sober alcoholics feel gratitude toward alcohol for the healing it ultimately brought them.

As we recognize that the people and situations we become angry about are just our projections of guilt away from ourselves, our prayer becomes:

Father, let me see the face of Christ instead of my mistakes. (Lesson 223)

TATION of him is VERY fearful. And you attack him still, to keep what seems to be YOURSELF unharmed. Yet in his hands IS your salvation. You see his madness, which you hate because you SHARE in it. And all the pity and forgiveness that would HEAL it gives way to fear. Brothers, you NEED forgiveness of each other for you will share in madness or in Heaven TOGETHER. And you will raise your eyes in FAITH together, or not at all.

Beside each of you is one who offers you the chalice of Atonement, for the Holy Spirit is in him. Would you hold his sins AGAINST him, or accept his gift to YOU? Is this giver of Salvation your friend or enemy? Choose which he is, remembering that you will RECEIVE of him according to your choice. He has IN HIM the power to forgive YOUR sins, as you for HIM. Neither can give it to himself alone. And yet your savior stands beside each one. Let him be what he IS, and seek not to make of love an enemy.

Behold your Friend, the Christ Who stands beside you. How holy and how beautiful He is! You THOUGHT He sinned, because you cast the veil of sin upon Him to HIDE His loveliness. Yet still He holds forgiveness out to you, to SHARE His holiness. This 'enemy,' this 'stranger' still offers you salvation as His Friend. The 'enemies' of Christ, the worshippers of sin, know not Whom they attack. This is your brother, crucified by sin, and waiting for release from pain. Would you not OFFER him forgiveness, when only he can offer it to you? (Urtext, T 19 L 4-7, "The Lifting of the Veil")

Quick Draw McAngry

As I struggled with my lessons involving anger and forgiveness, I was dismayed to realize how quickly I still became angry, especially in light of my sincere efforts to follow a spiritual life. It often felt as if I had no choice. But in reality this feeling of "no choice" was just another choice designed to mask my awareness of having made the choice to be angry. And I had chosen anger so often that it had become second nature. I had become "Quick Draw McAngry," the fastest gun at the "I'm OK, You're Not OK Corral." In his article "Let There Be Forever Undone What Temporarily Came Between Us,"[74] ACIM scholar Kenneth Wapnick uncovers the ego's strategy to use anger in this passage from Lesson 136 of the Course:

> "Replacing the word *anger* for *sickness*, we read the following exposé of the ego's tactics: *Anger* is not an accident. Like all defenses, it is an insane device for self-deception. . . Defenses are not unintentional, nor are they made without awareness. They are secret, magic wands you wave when truth appears to threaten what you would believe. They seem to be unconscious but because of the rapidity with which you choose to use them. . . But afterwards, your plan requires that you must forget you made it, so it seems to be external to your own intent; a happening beyond your state of mind, an outcome with a real effect on you, instead of one effected by yourself."
>
> (Lesson 136.2:1-2; 3:1-3; 4:3, italics Dr. Wapnick's)

I work to defuse this "instant anger response" by looking squarely at my anger with my witness consciousness, choosing to slow down, and memorizing steps 1-4 on page 109 to deal with anger in the moment. In the aftermath, as I begin to calm down, I have to be vigilant against entertaining thoughts about whatever tempted me to anger. My ego nature would prefer to bounce my grievances around in my head endlessly, "proving" how *right* I am and what a *victim* I am of whatever it was that angered me. At this point, I often find it helpful to put my thoughts in writing to be evaluated for truth later. (More about this in the chapter "Mental Healing Work.") Application of many of the daily Workbook lessons is also helpful for dissipating anger.

Anger seems to make my mind numb to the truth, yet lightning fast for retorts and analysis of others. The slowing down of anger still takes a great force of will for me. I do not always succeed before responding in some external way. When I fail to contain my anger, I apologize for whatever anger I expressed. And then I forgive myself.

Forgiveness is like a tomato—a nutritious ideal you cultivate for the great joy of eating it.

Ho'oponopono – Forgiveness Hawaiian Style

Kahuna Harry Uhane Jim[75] shares the Hawaiian knowledge that there are only two kinds of forgiveness: now or later. Jim explains ho'oponopono as a way to "make things right, to bring

---

[74] "The Lighthouse," newsletter of the Foundation for *A Course in Miracles*, September 2008.

[75] *The Wise Secrets of Aloha*, www.harryjimlomilomi.com

balance to things, to disengage from conflict and unforgiveness." Like waves rolling onto a beach, ho'oponopono *erases* the furrows of disagreement and releases its hold, so disharmony doesn't dam (and damn) the future. Ho'oponopono lets illusions go.

The process of ho'oponopono is very simple—just say, pray, or chant (to yourself):

- ♥ *I'm sorry.* (This does not relinquish authority or demean, but engages the authority of the God of Love over all circumstances that do not feel loving or peaceful. It also accepts responsibility and acknowledges whatever mistakes you made.)
- ♥ *Please forgive me.* (Affirms the desire to be released of involvement in any circumstance that does not reflect your true nature.)
- ♥ *Thank you. I love you.* (Lets go of how the issue will be resolved and expresses gratitude to God for handling now all circumstances experienced as not loving or not peaceful, in trust that the highest possible resolution for all involved will manifest. This also blesses anyone involved in the conflict for his or her role in helping you to reclaim peace.)

Projection Infection Subjected to New Direction

As I was working on this chapter I had an encounter with a person who is very well-suited to trigger my anger. *"X"* (finding my communication tedious and judging it irrelevant) deleted something I had written in a blog, with the complaint that I would not let it pass without responding. I was furious.

Who is well-suited to trigger our anger? Anyone with whom we have an attachment—whose actions or opinions we believe affect our happiness or well-being—often family members, friends, bosses, and other coworkers. The underlying truth is that the more we are "in someone else's business," the more easily that person can function as a trigger for us. Non-attachment (which can be learned) keeps us "in our own business."

After using some of the guidelines from this chapter, my angry feelings dissipated in about ten minutes. I continued applying forgiveness strategies whenever the incident came to mind. Over the next day I put my judgments about *X* on paper and turned them around, finding all opposite statements that were at least as true (more about this in the chapter "Mental Healing Work.") By reversing my judgments through this "turnaround" process I was able to take back my projections. I thus reframed the incident as an experience I called to myself for my own healing. This freed me to see clearly what the trigger was in the situation, and to continue communicating with *X* without just stirring the anger pot.

Example: *X* deletes my blog entry and complains that I can't be quiet and just let things be.

Projections (Judgments):

- *X* does not value my gifts.
- *X* is controlling.
- *X* is rude.
- *X* is lazy about the blog.

Turnarounds (Reverse statements at least as true as my judgments):

- I do not value my gifts when I need someone else to value them.
- *X* does value my gifts. (How can I know what is in *X*'s heart?)
- I do not value *X*'s gifts when I expect *X* to act to my specifications.
- I am controlling when I try to control *X*'s controlling behavior.
- I am rude when I angrily protest *X*'s rudeness.
- *X* is not lazy. (*X*'s schedule would "wipe out" a teenager on Red Bull.)
- I am lazy, and therefore don't want any fruit of my effort thrown away.

The fact that our projections come from our hidden judgments of ourselves explains why simply deciding not to be "judgmental" doesn't work. Forgiveness—specifically *self-forgiveness*—is required.

At the same time of the blog incident, I realized that three out of four hot water faucets in my home were leaking. Water symbolizes emotion and our homes are extensions of ourselves. Hot is associated with anger. I called a plumber, with a prayer that I had done enough of my healing work for the repairs to hold. They did.

> *Today I learn the law of love; that what I give my brother is my gift to me. . . . he whom I forgive will give me gifts beyond the worth of anything on earth. Let my forgiven brothers fill my store with Heaven's treasures, which alone are real. Thus is the law of love fulfilled.* (Lesson 344)

As I work with my anger, I realize that I have unleashed it most toward those I care most about. I have mistaken my attachment for part of my love. Indeed I *have* loved many people I have been angry with, but when I am in the state of anger I cannot be in the state of loving them. Anger is all about me: my judgments, my need for something from others, and my fear that I am not getting my needs met. Anger is about my vulnerability. Anger stains love. Thank God anger is temporary.

> *Judgment and love are opposites. From one comes all the sorrows of the world. But from the other comes the peace of God Himself.* (Lesson 352)

The greater the blame, the greater the pain

Would I accuse myself of doing this?. . .Would I condemn myself for doing this? (Lesson 134)

Because of the mechanism of projection, the above condemnation has already come to pass simply by virtue of seeing something objectionable in someone else. When I see something "wrong" with others, I have indeed already accused and condemned myself, then projected it outward. So the two questions above are not just theoretical inquiries as to whether I (having all the inside information that would lead to compassion) would assess the same guilt on myself as I do on others, without the benefit of such information. Of course I wouldn't. These two questions also function as practical advice.

First do no harm—to anyone.

Beware of the temptation to perceive yourself unfairly treated. (Urtext, T 26 K 4)

When I am focused on another's error, I burden myself emotionally in direct proportion to my outrage. If I am upset because of the treatment I am receiving, my level of pain is completely dependent upon my level of blame. When I am the jailer, I also become a prisoner. Regardless of projection, should I give pain to myself by accusing and condemning another? Should I punish myself for another's "offense"? No! Every charge I levy against another in my mind is heaped upon myself because I am steeped in it. This *exposure,* added to the guilt of projection, is what is painful. Nothing another can do to me can affect my peace and joy, because peace and joy are my birthright from God. I always ultimately hurt *myself* with my own thoughts. Should I thus condemn myself for the sins I am perceiving in another? No, not if I want peace. And peace is all I really want.

Anger is a self-destructive choice. Entertaining anger is like going to an ice cream parlor, gorging on the flavor du jour, and expecting the server to get fat. Anger "tastes good" in the moment, but there is a price to be paid. Anger can even become addictive.

Anger must come from judgment. Judgment is the weapon I would use against myself,
to keep the miracle [of complete forgiveness] *away from me.* (Lesson 347)

The following *Mastery Forgiveness Process* is particularly helpful for anger and any upsets "in the moment" before taking time to do deeper emotional work such as *Michael Mirdad's Healing/Forgiveness Process* (see the chapter "Emotional Healing Work.") The *Mastery Forgiveness Process* is also perfect to use as your issues become more healed (but not yet non-existent), and there is less need for great releases of emotional energy. This fast-moving process leads you easily through the crucial steps to practice conscious, complete forgiveness of yourself and others:

- ♥ identify your judgments,
- ♥ reclaim your projections,
- ♥ forgive all of it, and,
- ♥ reveal your innate compassion and love.

MASTERY FORGIVENESS PROCESS[76]

I choose to see my brother's sinlessness. . . . In him I find my Self. . .
Forgiveness lets me know that minds are joined. (Lessons 335, 336)

Principles for Review:

- ♥ You will project onto others what remains unhealed and unforgiven (judged) within yourself.
- ♥ Healing requires vigilance and discipline to observe yourself with honesty and innocence.
- ♥ Anger is never justified[77] (valid); all events are neutral, providing a chance to choose love.
- ♥ All actions and energies are love or the call for love.[78]
- ♥ You literally create everything you choose; nothing is forced upon you. The universe is conspiring *with you* to awaken *you* and heal *you*.
- ♥ Ask "what is *this moment* teaching me?"
- ♥ You are a conduit of energy that can flow so radiantly that the conduit becomes no barrier to Light.
- ♥ Judgment is contraction of this conduit. Judgment causes dissonant vibration and breaks down cellular structure. Furthermore, correct judgment is humanly impossible.[79]
- ♥ Forgiveness is relaxation, peace, trust, and faith.
- ♥ Past mistakes can be undone in the present because the energy exists now, and now is all there is. All minds are joined. We are spirit, not bodies.
- ♥ To heal *memories* of times you have judged others, say to yourself now:
  - o I judge you not.
  - o I extend forgiveness to myself for what I have created.
  - o I embrace you. I love you. I free you to be yourself. I bless you with the blessing of Christ.
  - o Then let the image dissolve into light until it is gone, and be done with it.

---

[76] Developed from "Healing Exercise," Lesson 3, The Power of Forgiveness, The Way of the Heart, *The Way of Mastery,* Shanti Christo Foundation. Use of this material is with the permission of the Shanti Christo Foundation.

[77] (Text, Chapter 30:VI. *"The Justification for Forgiveness"*)

[78] (Urtext, T 14 F 7)

[79] *The aim of our curriculum, unlike the goal of the world's learning, is the recognition that judgment in the usual sense is impossible. This is not an opinion but a fact. In order to judge anything rightly, one would have to be fully aware of an inconceivably wide range of things; past, present and to come. One would have to recognize in advance all the effects of his judgments on everyone and everything involved in them in any way. And one would have to be certain there is no distortion in his perception, so that his judgment would be wholly fair to everyone on whom it rests now and in the future. Who is in a position to do this? Who except in grandiose fantasies would claim this for himself?* (Manual for Teachers, 10. *"How is Judgment Relinquished?"*) Judgment is also addressed in Workbook Lessons 151, 154 and 311.

MASTERY FORGIVENESS PROCESS

1. **RECOGNIZE:** I am the source of my experience. I am feeling disturbed. What *in me* needs to be healed?

2. **RELAX:** Breathe deeply and rhythmically. Let the body soften and relax, then. . .

3. **ASK:** What is it *in the energy* of this *person* or this *situation* that is really upsetting to me?

4. **RECEIVE:** You will see it right away: _____

5. **RETRIEVE:** Ask: When have I done that to another? When have I held *the same energy*?

6. **CONNECT:** You will receive an answer or a memory. Continue to breathe deeply and relax. Look upon the energy. Honor it. Love it. For it is your creation, coming back to you that you might embrace and transform it. Stay with the answer or memory, saying:
   - ♥ Ah, being _____. Yes, I sure can be _____.
   - ♥ I've been that way in the past. I know that energy very well.

7. **FORGIVE YOURSELF:** Looking with deep honesty and sincerity upon a memory in which you have been _____, say to yourself:
   - ♥ I forgive me for being _____.
   - ♥ I forgive my judgment of myself.
   - ♥ I choose to teach only love.
   - ♥ Let the image dissolve and disappear from your mind.

8. **FORGIVE OTHERS:** Bring your awareness back to whatever upset you, and say (to yourself):
   - ♥ I forgive you, (insert name), for allowing the energy of _____ to temporarily make a home in your mind.
   - ♥ Holy Spirit, show me the innocent light within _____ (person or situation in the present that you have found upsetting).

9. **SEE CLEARLY:** When you see the light, ask:
   - ♥ What is this _____ energy in them masking? What are they really crying out for?

10. **LOVE:** You will feel compassion, for it will be revealed to you why they are hurting inside. Sit with this compassion and breathe it in. Accept it as part of yourself.

11. **CHOOSE AGAIN:** Now you are prepared to choose compassion instead of reaction. Ask that God's Will be done through you, and your words and behavior can be different than you ever have imagined.
    - ♥ *For through you will flow exactly what serves them.*

12. GIVE THANKS: To your Father and your brother, for leading you back to love.

Mastery Forgiveness Process: An example

The officers from the new security company employed by our condominium association were not meeting expectations. It seemed as though they had never done residential work before and they often displayed a lack of common sense for priorities and procedures. As the only actual resident serving on the board of our association, I felt responsible for making sure our security needs were met. With the goal of a successful working relationship, I began offering feedback to our officers. I was not usually angry when I began talking with an officer, but I often felt angry by the time we were done. So I began using the *Mastery Forgiveness Process* for these encounters. For example:

1. I RECOGNIZED: I am the source of my experience. I am feeling disturbed. What *in me* needs to be healed?

2. I RELAXED: Breathing deeply and rhythmically, I let my body soften and relax.

3. I ASKED: What is it *in the energy* of this *person* or this *situation* that is really pushing my buttons?

4. I RECEIVED: Every time I bring something up, Officer *X* interrupts me with rambling excuses instead of listening. *X* does not seem to care what I want.

5. I RETRIEVED: I asked, "When have I done that to another? When have I held *the same energy*?"

6. I CONNECTED: I remembered how easy it is for me to interrupt others. I used to interrupt someone I assisted when what he was saying felt threatening to me, which was often. The memory felt shameful in light of my current situation, but I continued to breathe deeply and relax. I looked upon the energy of *feeling threatened and interrupting* until I was able to honor and love it. For it was my creation, coming back to me that I might embrace and transform it. I stayed with the memory, saying:
   - ♥ Ah, feeling threatened and interrupting others. Yes, I sure can feel threatened and interrupt others.
   - ♥ I've been that way in the past. I know that energy very well.

7. I FORGAVE MYSELF: I looked at my memory of interrupting and said to myself:
   - ♥ I forgive me for feeling threatened and interrupting.
   - ♥ I forgive my judgment of myself.
   - ♥ I choose to teach only love. Then I let the image dissolve and disappear.

8. I FORGAVE OTHERS: I brought my awareness back to Officer *X* and said (to myself):
   - ♥ I forgive you, Officer *X*, for allowing the energy of feeling threatened and interrupting to temporarily make a home in your mind.
   - ♥ Holy Spirit, show me the innocent light within Officer *X*.

9. I SAW CLEARLY: When I saw Officer *X*'s light, I asked, "What is this 'feeling threatened and interrupting' energy in Officer *X* masking? What is he really crying out for?"
    - ♥ I could see that his self-esteem was not strong, and he was asking for love in the form of job security and positive feedback on his work.

10. I LOVED: Now I felt compassion for Officer *X*'s sense of vulnerability. I sat with my compassion and accepted it as part of me.

11. I CHOSE AGAIN: I decided to always remember to find something to praise before I offered corrective feedback. I asked that God's Will be done through me, then spoke with Officer *X*. I told him I had noticed improvement and appreciated it. I also asked him not to interrupt me and said he would have a chance to speak when I was through. The outcome was different than I could imagine while I was feeling angry and frustrated about being interrupted. Officer *X* and I agreed completely. We both felt heard and began to forge a partnership with the common goal of efficient and cordial security for our community.
    - ♥ *Through me flowed exactly what served him,* so Officer *X* was able to relax and serve us.

12. I GAVE THANKS: To my Father and my brother, Officer *X*, for leading me back to love.

This "nuts and bolts" forgiveness process continues to rescue me from insanity and return me to peace. It unravels complicated appearances and reminds me that I *am* as God created me.

Politesse

I am not the victim of the world I see. [And neither is anyone else.][80]

When we begin to understand that each of us is responsible for the events and quality of our own lives, it may seem to make sense to stop apologizing for things we say and do that others find hurtful. Aren't they responsible for their own experiences? Yes, they are. We are each responsible for our experiences in this Earth-dream called life. However, the most *loving* thing usually is to apologize when another seems to be hurt by our words or actions, especially when social convention would deem it so.

Apologizing is a loving act not necessarily because you are wrong, but because apologizing helps the other person find the foothold to practice forgiveness. Think of apologizing as a gentle hand to help another get his balance. And chances are that if there is a ripple of discontent between you, *something* you said or did was not entirely right or loving. Identify it and apologize.

Politeness, etiquette, and graciousness are woven with strands of Divine Light. We struggle enough learning to forgive. As some of us begin to really understand forgiveness, taking it to its highest spiritual level of focusing on Truth and letting go of illusion, we have an opportunity to

---
[80] (Lesson 31)

serve by creating an atmosphere conducive to helping others find this path. Therefore, let us practice humility and gentleness, and apologize freely.

> *The might of God's teachers lies in their gentleness, for they have understood their evil thoughts came neither from God's Son nor his Creator. Thus did they join their thoughts with Him Who is their Source.*
> (Manual for Teachers, 4. *"What Are the Characteristics of God's Teachers?"*)

> [Forgiveness is] *the altar to One God, One Father, One Creator, and One Thought,* [where] *we stand together as one Son of God. Not separate from Him Who is our Source; not distant from one brother. . . , we stand in blessedness, and give as we receive. The Name of God is on our lips. And as we look within, we see the purity of Heaven shine in our reflection of our Father's Love.*

> *. . . We would behold it* [innocence] *shining with the grace of God in everyone. We would not have it be withheld from anything we look upon. And to ensure this holy sight is ours, we offer it to everything we see.* (Lesson 187)

In some circumstances we do not have access to a person to be able to apologize, or doing so might now be intrusive or upsetting. But we can still receive the gifts of giving apology.

Apology Exercise:

Think of someone to whom you have not given an adequate apology—someone you have helped propel along the path of pain with your actions or omissions. Get clear on the essence of what you did with your action or inaction—did you attack, betray, belittle, or neglect this child of God? How would your decision have been felt by them? Own the essence of your action, then picture the other person clearly in your mind. Picture them looking into your eyes; see their eyes with your mind's eye. Now, with God at your side, look into their eyes and offer your simple words of apology. Imagine all tension between you melting and all agendas evaporating as two Sons of God simply face each other in truth. Feel the release of forgiveness pouring over both of you. See the love in your brother's eyes as he accepts your apology. Allow him to give you a message—with his eyes, his touch, or his voice. Savor this holy instant of peace between you, and give thanks.

~ ~ ~

> *Let me perceive forgiveness as it is.* [I forgive illusions, not truth.] (Lesson 134)

The bottom line is that all I am ever being called to forgive is a "dream." No matter how evil (vile or veiled) the person or situation may appear, when it happens in this world, it hasn't *really* happened. There is NOTHING "out there" that I find objectionable that is not some aspect of myself I have subconsciously judged and rejected. If I go to sleep and have a dream that I am wronged, is it not insane to retaliate when I am awakened? And who hurt me in the dream? Was it not myself, the dreamer of the dream?

You make [project] *what you defend against,*
and by your own defense against it [anger and attack] *is it real and inescapable.*
Lay down your arms, and only then do you perceive it false. (Lesson 170)

I have no cause for anger or for fear, for You surround me.
And in every need that I perceive, Your grace suffices me.[81] (Lesson 348)

The illusion is not real, and I am safe within God always. God's grace provides everything I need to fulfill His Will of happiness for me, which I accept as my own. To claim my happiness:

[I am willing] *to let forgiveness rest upon all things without exception and without reserve.*
(Workbook, Part II, 9. *"What is the Second Coming?"*)

Forgive everything—that is all that matters! Once I realign my thinking with the truth, my whole being resonates forgiveness:

Peace fills my heart, and floods my body with the purpose of forgiveness. (Lesson 267)

And so it is.

---

[81] *Philip saith unto him, Lord, shew us the Father, and it sufficeth us.* (John 14:8)

Past and Future

I loose the world from all I thought it was. (Lesson 132)

Rainbow Obsidian

Past and Future

I loose the world from all I thought it was. (Lesson 132)

Past and Future

The past is over. It can touch me not. (Lesson 289)

All your past except its beauty is gone, and nothing is left except a blessing.[82]

When my mind is focused on the past I am seeing only ghosts—illusions of illusions.[83]

Unless the past is over in my mind, the real world must escape my sight. For I am really looking nowhere; seeing but what is not there. How can I then perceive the world forgiveness offers? This the past was made to hide, for this the world that can be looked on only now. It [the forgiven world] *has no past. For what can be forgiven but the past, and if it is forgiven it is gone. . . . Here is the end of guilt. . . . the end of all . . . dreams and all . . . pain.* (Lesson 289)

The world believes that the past predicts the future. The Course makes clear that this belief is wrong. Instead, the present extends into the future.[84] From peace today comes peace tomorrow. The past is irrelevant, unless we drag it along. We free ourselves of the past by releasing judgment and practicing forgiveness.

I seek a future different from the past. . . . [Without judgment] *the future now is recognized as but extension of the present,* [the past having no effects]. *. . . Who can grieve or suffer when the present has been freed, extending its security and peace into a quiet future filled with joy?* (Lesson 314)

This passage may not seem to apply if you are mourning the loss of a "golden" past, but it does. The joy and beauty perceived in yesterday are the past to be left behind. All the love you created in these experiences has been saved for you by God in the *"storehouse of treasures."*[85]

---

[82] (Text, Chapter 5:IV.8.2)

[83] *I see only the past. . . .Old ideas about time are very difficult to change, because everything you believe is rooted in time, and depends on your not learning these new ideas about it. Yet that is precisely why you need new ideas about time. This first time idea is not really so strange as it may sound at first.*

Look at a cup, for example. Do you see a cup, or are you merely reviewing your past experiences of picking up a cup, being thirsty, drinking from a cup, feeling the rim of a cup against your lips, having breakfast and so on? Are not your aesthetic reactions to the cup, too, based on past experiences? How else would you know whether or not this kind of cup will break if you drop it? What do you know about this cup except what you learned in the past? You would have no idea what this cup is, except for your past learning. Do you, then, really see it? (Lesson 7)

[84] Within the illusion of time. Reality or Heaven— our state of being within God—is eternal, making concepts of past, present, and future meaningless.

[85] *We have referred many times in the text to the storehouse of treasures laid up equally for the giver and the receiver of God's gifts. Not one is lost, for they can but increase.* (Manual for Teachers, 7. *"Should Healing Be Repeated?"*)

But your grief *today* over their loss extends into the future. Suspend your judgment that today should be like the "golden days" that have passed. Then forgive everything that brought you here, and you have reclaimed peace—for today and the future.

Manawa – Now is the moment of power.
—Hawaiian Shamanic Principle[86]

Although you have freed your present, the past may seem to creep back as your grief or issues pop up again. This resurfacing is an attempt by the ego to thwart healing. The ego is in effect saying to you, the decision maker, "DON'T YOU *DARE* CHANGE YOUR THINKING!" Yet nothing is amiss with the healing you have already done if it resulted in your peace. Issues resurfacing just indicate that the present needs to be freed from the past *again*, like weeding a garden. Persistence pays great dividends in progress, and patience will someday yield perfection.

Loss now is likely to bring back to mind other times of loss—past events when you felt the same way. Making these associations with the past is important to your present healing. Otherwise, memories of past losses are not helpful, except perhaps for making amends. Impulses to reactivate the past for any other purpose are detrimental to your present healing. Trips down memory lane remove you from the eternal now and tend to place your focus on others, removing it from healing yourself. Reactivating the past places you squarely in distraction or projection.

All things are lessons God would have me learn. (Lesson 193)

Let the past be part of today's lesson, and then move on.

If I defend myself I am attacked.
But in defenselessness I will be strong,
and I will learn what my defenses hide. (Lesson 135)

[Defense] gives illusions full reality, and then attempts to handle them as real. It adds illusions to illusions, thus making correction doubly difficult. And it is this you do when you attempt to plan the future, activate the past, or organize the present as you wish. . . .

What could you not accept, if you but knew that everything that happens, all events, past, present and to come, are gently planned by One Whose only purpose is your good? Perhaps you have misunderstood His plan, for He would never offer pain to you. But your defenses did not let you see His loving blessing shine

[86] as related by Serge Kahili King in *Urban Shaman*.

in every step you ever took. While you made plans for death, He led you gently to eternal life.

Your present trust in Him is the defense that promises a future undisturbed, without a trace of sorrow, and with joy that constantly increases, as this life becomes a holy instant, set in time, but heeding only immortality. Let no defenses but your present trust direct the future, and this life becomes a meaningful encounter with the truth that only your defenses would conceal.

Without defenses, you become a light. . . . And it will lead you on in ways appointed for your happiness according to the ancient plan, begun when time was born. . . .

We make no plans for how it will be done, but realize that our defenselessness is all that is required for the truth to dawn upon our minds with certainty. . . .

If there are plans to make you will be told of them. They may not be the plans you thought were needed, nor indeed the answers to the problems which you thought confronted you. . . .

Try not to shape this day as you believe would benefit you most. For you can not conceive of all the happiness that comes to you without your planning. Learn today. . . . Throughout the day, as foolish little things appear to raise defensiveness in you and tempt you to engage in weaving plans, remind yourself. . .:

. . . I will not defend myself, because the Son of God needs no defense against the truth of his reality. (Lesson 135)

Relax into the peace and possibility of the present moment.

This instant is the only time there is.
. . . in this instant has forgiveness come to set me free. (Lesson 308)

In fearlessness and love I spend today. This day, my Father, would I spend with You. . . .
And what I will experience is not of time at all. (Lesson 310)

I heal the past so I can use the present to be free. In this freedom *I place the future in the Hands of God.*[87]

I seek a future different from the past. . . . [Without judgment] *the future now is recognized as but extension of the present,* [the past having no effects]. (Lesson 314)

---

[87] (Lesson 194)

Since time and space are mere constructs of the illusory world of form,[88] we can even function as our own angels. Part of my exercise routine is stair-climbing. I walk to a nearby parking garage and climb 13 flights to the top where I can see cityscapes spread out around me. The highlight of my walk, I love to send out prayers and blessings in the four directions as I circle the perimeter of the roof, taking in the breeze and the beautiful view. For a time I was inspired to send prayers of love, light, strength, protection, and healing back through time to myself in the most troubled period of my youth. I invited that frightened and confused young girl to rest in my open arms and share my joyful heart. For years I have been aware that angels and light beings brought me through that difficult period. And one day up on the roof, as I sent my prayers, I realized that I myself was one of those angels.

Time is not real. You, too, can do this with your past. Simply hold in your mind a vision of yourself as you once were, like a snapshot. Then extend your love and elevated consciousness of now back through time to yourself. Promise to hold your former self up until you make it here to the present. Envision cradling your past self in your arms, like a beloved child.

. . . Love is ever-present, here and now. (Lesson 308)

---

[88] *Acts were not necessary before the Separation, because the time-space belief did not exist.* (Urtext, T 2 B 41)

Emotional Healing Work

I am as God created me. I am God's Son.
Today I lay aside all sick illusions of myself,
and let my Father tell me Who I really am. (Lesson 120)

Chrysocolla

Emotional Healing Work

I am as God created me. I am God's Son.
Today I lay aside all sick illusions of myself,
and let my Father tell me Who I really am. (Lesson 120)

Emotional Healing Work

Emotional healing work builds a foundation for practicing forgiveness. It lays aside our sick self-image so that we may open to embodying our true, God-given nature. We forgive by acknowledging *our* issues, accepting responsibility, releasing our painful emotions, and cultivating the peace of God—we empty ourselves of pain and refill with God. In the context of healing loss, we can look at emotional healing work as a choice not to hoard grief. Instead we allow grief energy to move through us, and then pour love into the empty space.

Based on the principles of *A Course in Miracles* and his vast counseling experience, Dr. Michael Mirdad has developed a simple process for healing with forgiveness. Once understood, we can easily practice this method on ourselves or on others. I developed the *Mirdad Healing/ Forgiveness Process* worksheet found at the end of this chapter as a guide to keep myself on track while awash in the emotions of doing my own healing work.

Healing occurs when we release that which impedes us (human emotions, attitudes, and beliefs) and refill with that which exalts us (peace, love, joy, safety, and abundance—the state God Wills for His Son). In order to effect lasting change in ourselves, we must both release what doesn't work AND refill with what does. We're like a pitcher of that colored powdered punch mix for kids, made per package instructions. The punch mix represents our woundedness; the water represents God. Made in the image of God, we are a pitcher of pure water. Entertaining the idea of separation from God, we dreamed up sin, guilt, and fear, adding the powder to our pitcher of pure water. Each time we accomplish healing, we pour out some of the colored punch and replace it with the pure, clear water of God. Thus the pitcher of punch becomes more and more dilute, until eventually it's again indistinguishable from pure water. But unlike actual punch, this *healing* punch tastes better and better as it's watered down!

To heal—to release your woundedness around an issue and refill your consciousness with the pure water of God—do the worksheet in a quiet place where you will not be interrupted with other matters. Choose a safe area where you will be free to cry or express other emotions. Although this work adapts well to a healing session with a coach, counselor, or trusted friend who understands the process, it can also easily be done alone. At its heart the work is a sacred healing encounter between you and God, so it should be respected and given proper time and privacy. Your investment in this healing work is visionary—seeing beyond the present moment—and the ultimate reward is priceless peace and joy.

It's important not do this work around others as a means of communicating your concerns to them. The time for communicating is after you have done your healing work and are feeling calm and peaceful. Often you will no longer feel the need to communicate much of what seemed so pressing before.

Step One. I RECOGNIZE: (the manifested version of the problem – facts, situations, opinions)

List the components of an issue that is upsetting you. If you need to, journal freely on a separate sheet of paper. Then use those results to clarify and condense the problem as you see it. But work only on one issue at a time. In healing you need to be selective to be effective. Save your feelings for Step Two. In Step One describe the situation from your point of view—your *most self-serving* point of view. Don't exaggerate, but don't "pull punches" and get "spiritual" at this point. Be blunt, especially with any personal opinions you may be inclined to judge or censor. Be childish, petty, a victim, whatever fits. Your point of view is fueling your upset and needs to be seen and dealt with at this stage—by YOU. If you have trouble accessing your judgmental opinions, download and fill in Byron Katie's *Judge-Your-Neighbor Worksheet*[89] and use it for Step One.

An example of Step One:

1. I recognize: I expect *X* to apologize to me. *X* should be honest and aware and realize how she wronged me. *X* betrayed me. *X* should not have pushed me out of her life. If *X* cared for me, she would apologize. If *X* were walking her talk, she would apologize.

Step Two. I ACCEPT: I am feeling _____, and I am responsible for my emotions:

Now it's time to enumerate the *feelings* that *you* have about everything listed in Step One. The top row of the table below contains the four basic negative emotions. Underneath them are some variations of the four basic negative emotions:

Four Basic Negative Emotions Make You SAAG

Sad	Angry	Afraid	Guilty
Depressed	Frustrated	Jealous	Ashamed
Hurt	Irritated	Lonely	Embarrassed
Down	Suspicious	Anxious	Stupid
Overwhelmed	Disgusted	Vulnerable	Bad
Exhausted	Smug	Shy	Responsible

You may think of other words that more precisely express degrees and nuances of the above-listed feelings, but distill these other words down to one of the four basic negative emotions. Look for the feelings underlying the feelings, until you have reached the basic emotion involved. In the language of emotional healing, extensive vocabulary is just confusing. In truth, all of the myriad of problems human beings experience in the emotional arena boil down to one core issue, the belief that we are separate from God. A few soul-level issues arise from this false belief of separation, and a few basic negative emotions arise from these soul issues. All of the other painful emotions, and the intricate specifics in our lives, are just symbolic of the one core issue— the belief that we are separate from God.

How the wide spectrum of painful emotions springs from the single false belief in separation from God can be illustrated by the way all colors derive from white light bent through a prism:

---

[89] Byron Katie's *Judge-Your-Neighbor Worksheet* is available at www.thework.com .

White Light	No color	God
- - - - - Bent through	a prism - - - - - -	Idea of Separation
Red Yellow Blue	Primary Colors	Soul Issues
Orange Green Violet	Secondary Colors	Basic Negative Emotions
256 Color Palette and beyond	Full Color Spectrum	Emotional Nuances

New items for Step One may come up as you identify your feelings. Add them there.

In Step Two we are claiming only *our* feelings. Feelings can differ greatly from different points of view. Consider an abandoned, condemned building that is being demolished. It's a tragedy for any small animals, addicts, or homeless people who are inside or use this building. It's "just a job" to the workers doing the detonation. For neighbors, it's a relief to be rid of an eyesore and source of problems. For the developers who will erect something else in its place, it's a beginning, a time of hope. If seen from an airplane, however, it's just a curiosity. And from the vantage point of outer space, it's so small it's nothing.

An example of Step Two:

2. I accept: I am feeling angry, sad, and afraid that I am not important enough to be loved. I am feeling guilty that I caused this, and I am responsible for my emotions:

My issue is greater than it appears; I have felt this way before: (people, situations from the past)

Continuing the example in Step Two:

My issue is greater than it appears; I have felt this way before: I felt angry, sad, afraid, and guilty when I was sent from my home to live with relatives at age 15.

This issue triggers my soul issues of: (Separate, Guilty, Afraid, Unworthy, Unlovable, Empty)

Separate	Guilty	Afraid	Unworthy	Unlovable	Empty
Sad	Sad	Sad	Sad	Sad	Sad
Angry	Angry	Angry	Angry	Angry	Angry
Afraid	Afraid		Afraid	Afraid	Afraid
Guilty		Guilty	Guilty	Guilty	Guilty

Notice how the four basic negative emotions (sad, angry, afraid, and guilty) are translations of the soul issues (separate, guilty, afraid, unworthy, unlovable, and empty, shown in the top shaded row). You will decide whether your sadness in a particular situation relates to soul issues of feeling guilty, unworthy, unlovable, or empty, and so on. You may identify more than one soul issue for each basic emotion. But you can be assured that "separate" is *always* an underlying soul issue of any basic negative emotion, and that "anger" always boils down to "afraid," and possibly other soul issues.

> Continuing the example in Step Two, soul issues:

> This triggers my soul issues of Guilty, Afraid, Unlovable, Empty, and Separate. My anger over my perception of being betrayed and rejected is much deeper and more far-reaching than it appears on the surface. It literally rattles my peace, safety, and worthiness. While it may be uncomfortable, the potential to reveal and heal my soul issues makes the situation profoundly *valuable* to me.

Take plenty of time to work on Steps One and Two. Cry freely when you feel tears welling up, pound pillows or scream into a pillow to vent your anger, etc. Be creative *within the context of safety for yourself and others*. Give yourself permission to have an emotional "tantrum" and resist any urge to stop and "button everything up" too soon. However, ALWAYS DO ALL FIVE STEPS in one sitting, even if it means not fully exploring and releasing everything in Steps One and Two. You can revisit the issues later. It is important to release AND refill in each sitting because BOTH releasing and refilling are necessary for healing. Refilling distinguishes *healing* from simply releasing or venting. Releasing alone usually makes people feel better for a time, but the feeling of well-being does not last because nothing has really changed. The punch (the issue) does not get diluted because no pure water (God essence) has been added.

When you're done with Steps One and Two (or almost out of time), do the prayer work in Step Three.

Step Three. I surrender the whole issue to You, God, for healing and transformation.

Prayerfully name and surrender the general issue that is troubling you, identified in Steps One and Two, such as "my anger about _____" or "my fear about _____." Name and surrender the soul issues you have identified in Step Two. Then affirm:

God, I trust You will take my upset from me. I don't know how to handle it, but You do.

This prayer is an effective way to "turn it over," as is widely practiced in the 12 Step tradition and many other spiritual practices. Declare that you will "let go and let God" in conscious awareness of *what* you are letting go. But as you pray, even things you do not fully understand can be surrendered. Understand what you can, then give it *all* to God.

> Continuing the example with Step Three:

> Father, I surrender my anger, my sadness, and my fear about not receiving an apology from *X*. I surrender my upset about not receiving apologies in general, and I surrender my anger, sadness, fear, and guilt from when I was 15. I give to You my soul issues of Guilty, Afraid, Unlovable, Empty, and Separate. I trust You will take them from me. I don't know how to handle them, but You do.

Step Four. I refill with God.

Choose two aspects[90] of God from the list that follows that feel appropriate to the work you have just done:

Peace	Healing	Wholeness
Love	Forgiveness	Hope
Self-worth	Joy	Bliss
Safety	Clarity	

Now, while sitting or lying comfortably with eyes closed and spine straight, refill meditatively using the following method:

Inhale: As you inhale into your heart center (chakra), repeat the two chosen words to yourself, feeling their meaning. You are drawing these qualities from God and the Heavens through the top of your head (crown chakra) down into your heart. Then pause and hold your breath for just a moment, as if to implant the essence of the words in your heart. This pause accomplishes "anchoring" of the essence.

Exhale: As you exhale, spread the essence of the chosen words to every cell of your body while you silently affirm "and so it is."

Repeat the inhale/exhale cycle as above about 12 times.

Step Five. I give thanks for the healing I have received.

Now give thanks to God for the healing you have just received—and that it is so easy to do.

> Continuing the example with Steps Four and Five:
>
> I refill with love and self-worth, and close by giving thanks.

If, after going through the Healing/Forgiveness Process, you are still feeling emotionally or energetically out of balance, try a cycle or two of the energy-balancing Emotional Freedom Technique (EFT®).[91] And then go upon your way—happier, lighter, and closer to God and your true Self.

Repeat *Michael Mirdad's Healing/Forgiveness Process* as necessary. Doing it several or *many* times on a particular issue does not mean the healing work was ineffective. It is merely an indication of how much emotional "stuff" you were able to access and release. Just keep doing

---

[90] God, being One, cannot truly have aspects or facets. But in the world of illusion there seem to be several qualities that describe God. They are all the same, and all beyond description, but these nuances of language can help us reunite what we believe has been shattered.

[91] Complete instructions for this simple tapping technique developed by Gary Craig can be found online for free at www.emofree.com .

forgiveness work with faith that it will heal core emotional issues. Do the work of forgiveness on all matters that upset you, whether or not they seem to pertain to your loss.

Directions for using the turnaround portion of *Michael Mirdad's Healing/Forgiveness Process* worksheet are given in the next section on "Mental Healing Work."

Mourning is Broken

Notice that mourning exercises the four basic negative emotions—sad, angry, afraid, and (often) guilty. Thus mourning is clearly a manifestation of our core soul issues—separate, guilty, afraid, unworthy, unlovable, and empty. Just as the ego opposes and imagines a place where God is not, our soul issues and negative emotions oppose the Heavenly consciousness of peace, love, joy, abundance, and safety we want to remember and embody. To mourn (or protest) tragic events such as 911, war, massacres, catastrophes, The Holocaust, slavery, the European conquest of the Americas, planned obsolescence, global warming, corporate greed, and so on, only feeds the negative energies that created these unfortunate events in the first place.

Lead Us Not Into Temptation

Don't lead yourself into sadness, depression, or guilt over the past. Such feelings only hinder you, your energy, and the energies of the involved souls who have passed on. We can create only at the energetic level we inhabit; therefore, if we want a more joyous and loving world we must step up and become more joyous and loving people. Hanging on to mourning misuses our love. A black armband cuts off the circulation of the living arm! If you are inspired to mark a tragic occasion, instead of mourning, *honor* the people, souls, cultures, bravery, beliefs, innocence, etc., of whatever was lost.

Practice Positive Remembrance

To honor, instead of mourn, practice positive remembrance. Choose to focus on the positive. Take positive action, celebrate positive qualities, and claim in yourself the positive aspects of whomever or whatever was lost.

For example, if you want to mark 911, focus on what was positive in the lives of any loved ones you may have lost. Were they dedicated and thoughtful co-workers? Brave rescuers? Loving partners? Nurturing parents? Trusted friends? Were they funny, talented, smart, loyal, thoughtful, sensitive, beautiful, sweet, faithful, etc.? Connect with these qualities in yourself—*you* also have them. Appreciate your lost loved one for mirroring these characteristics of love to you. Even if you did not personally know anyone directly affected, honor the bravery, dedication, love, sensitivity, and thoughtfulness of those who passed and that survivors displayed to one another in the aftermath of the tragedy. Consciously practice *in your own life* these admirable qualities that seem to have been lost. Love, in all its glorious variations, did not die with the body of your loved one.

When you practice positive remembrance, you help to transmute the negative energies that construct tragedies, making them less likely to occur. The ultimate honoring happens as you walk forward in your day-to-day life making loving choices. To honor all the children of God who have passed from this Earth, choose love now.

Should I really go there? Again?

You can't afford *not* to process your emotions until you can't afford to process your emotions. In other words, it is necessary to continue processing and healing wounds until such a high level of healing has been reached that processing would result *only* in losing focus from even higher goals. This paradoxical tipping point is a level determined by your spiritual advancement—how well you remember the Truth while living within the illusion—the waking version of "lucid dreaming." There is a point, after enough healing, when it is time to say, as did Jesus (when he spent 40 days and 40 nights fasting in the wilderness), *"Away from me all tempting thoughts!"*[92] But by this time you will be THOROUGHLY familiar with the emotions that are trying to surface—their pattern, their origin, their significance, and most importantly, their unreality.

Remember that choking back an emotion is *not* an indication that you understand it is not real. And denying an emotion is *not* thorough familiarity. For most of us the time to stop processing has not yet come. Thus we continue to "go there again," willing to take the steps to heal our painful emotions responsibly as they arise.

While "going there again," hold no judgments about your core wounds—they are merely symptoms of the dis-ease of separation, just as cravings are symptoms of the dis-ease of addiction. As long as you have a body, your wounds will likely surface from time to time. This recurrence does not negate your healing work thus far; it simply reflects the basic premise of the illusion—"I am separate from God."

---

[92] *The Aquarian Gospel of Jesus the Christ.* Also recorded in the Bible as, *"Get thee behind me, Satan."* (Luke 4:8)

Michael Mirdad's Healing/Forgiveness Process

1. I recognize: (Describe the manifested version of the problem—facts, situations, opinions.)

2. I accept: I am feeling _____ and I am responsible for my emotions. (Condense down to the four basic negative emotions: **sad, angry, afraid, guilty.** Uncover the emotion underlying anger.)

My issue is greater than it appears; I have felt this way before: (people, events from the past)

This issue triggers my core soul issues of: (separate, guilty, afraid, unworthy, unlovable, empty)

3. I surrender the whole issue to You, God, for healing and transformation.

I trust You will take my upset from me. I don't know how to handle it, but You do.

4. I refill with (aspects or facets of God):

(inhale into heart center, anchor, exhale, and spread to every cell of your body for 12 cycles)

List <u>Turnarounds</u> of Step 1 here AFTER completing Steps 1-5.

Peace
Love
Self-worth
Safety
Healing
Forgiveness
Joy
Clarity
Wholeness
Hope
Bliss

5. I give thanks for the healing I have received.

Mental Healing Work

I am determined to see things differently. (Lesson 21)

Fluorite

Mental Healing Work

I am determined to see things differently. (Lesson 21)

Mental Healing Work

The All is Spirit. The All is Mind. All is in the Mind of the All. The All is infinite and nothing really exists outside of Mind. The All is changeless. The All is life. The All is in all, and all is in the All.
    —The Law of Mind, Hermetic Laws of the Universe, as related by Michael Mirdad

"THE ALL" is Infinite Living Mind—the illumined call it SPIRIT!
    —The Hermetic Principle of Mentalism, *The Kybalion*

And what are grapes? They are but certain kinds of thought made manifest,
    and I can manifest that thought, and water will be wine.
        —Jesus, *The Aquarian Gospel of Jesus the Christ*

For as he thinketh in his heart, so is he. (Proverbs 23:7)

Thought creates, and the mind never sleeps.

. . .the source of healing. . . is in our minds because our Father placed it there for us. It is not farther from us than ourselves. It is as near to us as our own thoughts; so close it is impossible to lose.   (Lesson 140)

Thought creates hell, and thought creates heaven. Therefore, scrap your painful thoughts and trade up to thinking with God in the language of unconditional love. Do mental healing work to correct the errors in your thinking. You can't change how you feel without changing how you think. You can't change how you think without seeing your thoughts clearly and making different choices. The ego mind will be evasive and obstinate. Be gentle with yourself but firm in your goal not to believe the thoughts the ego will advocate to you.

Makia – Energy flows where attention goes.
    —Hawaiian Shamanic Principle[93]

Egoic thinking habits die hard not only because the ego is invested in its point of view, but also because old patterns die hard. Only after immersing myself in the work of forgiveness did I realize the formidable power of my *history* of negative thought. I became aware that I am inclined to frame even the most seemingly trivial and innocuous thoughts in negative terms. For example, one morning while cleaning my expensive glasses, I remembered how they had originally been drilled incorrectly so that they were prone to literally falling apart in my hands.

---

[93] as related by Serge Kahili King in *Urban Shaman.*

The problem had been corrected, at no additional cost to me, in two repairs over the course of a year. That morning I felt *grateful*—for the repairs and that I had nice glasses to wear. But I noticed that when the need to repair those glasses came into my memory, I also slipped off on a negative tangent of thought about "incompetent work nowadays." Thank God I noticed! Because *then* I was able to bring my thoughts back to focus on the positive—my gratitude to the optician, who had graciously made sure that my glasses were perfect, very likely at the cost of his own profit, and my gratitude for owning a pair of attractive, functional, high-end glasses.

> *I have no neutral thoughts. . . .*
> *Every thought you have contributes to truth or to illusion;*
> *either it extends the truth or it multiplies illusions.* (Lesson 16)

Faith did not "cure" me of negative thinking. Practice is changing my thinking. Vigilance for the truth, with intention toward positive thinking and rigorous self-observation to catch and correct negative thinking, creates new patterns. Every time I choose forgiveness, trust, or optimism, I etch the pattern of love more deeply into my experience and soul. I have no neutral thoughts—my thoughts are either part of the solution (Truth and Love) or part of the problem (the fear-filled illusion). I support the solution or the problem by exercising "solution" thoughts or "problem" thoughts.

> *. . . it is a fact that there are no private thoughts.* (Lesson 19)

I am thought because God is Thought, and I am created in the image of God. God is within me and I am within God. I have no private thoughts because I am joined with God and the collective Son of God, eternally part of the Oneness of God's creation. As I heal my thoughts I lift up my brothers. My "personal" healing is a service to all.

> *Healed perception becomes the means by which the Son of God*
> *forgives his brother and thus forgives himself.* (Lesson 43)

Exercise: To get a feel for how deeply habits are ingrained, move a clock in your home or workspace that you are *accustomed* to looking at out of visual range from where it used to be. Notice how long you keep checking the time in the old location. If you don't use clocks, move a wastebasket. It has been observed that it takes 21-30 days to break or establish habits. How long is this habit of yours persisting? Are your habits of thought less persistent, or more?

> *It is your thoughts alone that cause you pain. Nothing external to your mind can hurt or injure you in any way. . . . No one but yourself affects you. There is nothing in the world that has the power to make you ill or sad, or weak or frail. But it is you who have the power to dominate all things you see by merely recognizing what you are. As you perceive the harmlessness in them, they will accept your holy will as theirs. And what was seen as fearful now becomes a source of innocence and holiness.* (Lesson 190:5)

Read: *Loving What Is* by Byron Katie

Through what is called "Inquiry" or "The Work," Byron Katie lights the path away from the suffering caused by our erroneous thoughts. She clearly and lovingly shows us how to see what is not true in our thinking and offers a simple way to expand our thoughts to more fully embrace the truth. A wealth of information, including a book excerpt and worksheets, is available free of charge at her website: www.thework.com .

Complete Katie's *Judge-Your-Neighbor Worksheet* or *One-Belief-At-A-Time Worksheet* for issues that disturb your peace. Ask "the four questions" of each statement:

1. Is it true?
2. Can you absolutely know that it's true?
3. How do you react, what happens, when you believe that thought?
4. Who would you be without the thought?

Then apply the "turnaround," creating statements that are opposite to your judgments but at least as true.

Sit Down, Turnaround, Heal a Pile o' Thinkin'

Using Katie's turnarounds is a beautifully simple way to allow your mind to consider taking back its projections. Approach turnarounds like an exercise, without attachment. You are not committing to anything, just considering if some other statements might be at least as true, or truer, than judgments you have made.

Your judgments will appear in Step One of *Michael Mirdad's Healing/Forgiveness Process* worksheet as statements about others, such as:

- *X should be more loving*, should not have died/left, shouldn't talk to me like that. . .
- *X doesn't care about me*, didn't get a fair shake, is rude, is inconsiderate, is wrong. . .
- I need *X to respect me*, to come back, to apologize, to see that I am right. . .

The turnaround takes such statements and converts them to opposites, or reverts criticisms back to ourselves. For example, using the italicized judgments above, the turnaround yields:

- *X* shouldn't be more loving. (Whatever is *should* be, because it is. And who am I to dictate how things should be? Are other people, events and things my business, their business, or God's business?)
- I should be more loving. (When I am judging and criticizing *X*, I am not loving.)

- *X* does care about me. (Actions can betray our feelings. How can I really know what is in *X*'s heart? What other ways does *X* demonstrate caring about me?)
- I don't care about *X*. (When I am upset with *X* and dictating *X*'s life, how caring am I?)

- I don't need *X* to respect me. (I don't need anything from anyone when I claim my identity as a child of God.)
- I need to respect *X*. (I need to allow *X* to be herself, taking her journey at her own pace, in her own way.)

Katie's worksheets can be used to create Step One on *Michael Mirdad's Healing/ Forgiveness Process* worksheet. Whether using Katie's worksheet for Step One or writing freestyle, when you are through with Steps One through Five, apply the turnaround to your judgments from Step One.

I can elect to change all thoughts that hurt. (Lesson 284)

A friend who seemed to have no capacity to apologize handled a situation poorly and behaved hurtfully to me many times, and I struggled with immense anger over it. I could not manage to escape my thoughts of how I had been mistreated, as the "facts" seemed to support this idea. I would forgive one thing, and soon another painful memory would pop up in my mind to take its place. Finally, I used the tool of the turnaround to take back my many projections. As I owned the truth that I had made all the errors I experienced at the hand of my friend, I *joined* with him. This joining allowed my heart to expand into compassion and forgiveness for both of us, and I was able to release everything in a decree:

I no longer care what you did, or what you ever say or don't say about it.
I no longer care how you treat me.
I no longer care if you seem blind to your mistakes; I will not be blind to my own.
I forgive my lies, and I release you from yours.
I forgive my hypocrisy, and I release you from yours.
I forgive my callousness, and I release you from yours.
I forgive my vindictiveness, and I release you from yours.
I forgive my blindness, and I release you from yours.
I forgive my pride, and I release you from yours.
I forgive my error, and I release you from yours.
I forgive my fear, and I release you from yours.

Father, I trust that You will not allow me to be annihilated and I release the part of me that believes I can be hurt—my imaginary, separate, tiny self. In the Name of Love I take my place within the infinite circle that is You, All That Is, calling to my brother to join us in peace.

. . .he whom I forgive will give me gifts beyond the worth of anything on earth. (Lesson 344)

Study: *A Course in Miracles*[94]

Study the Text of *A Course in Miracles* enough to have a good general idea of what it says. Then do the Workbook lessons, which lead you in practice of the Course. However, the text is over 600 pages of what can be arduous reading. If you are not familiar with what the Course says (and even if you are), reading about it can be very helpful. The following are some excellent overviews of the Course:

Gloria and Kenneth Wapnick – *Awaken From the Dream* – www.facim.org
Jon Mundy – *Living A Course in Miracles* – www.miraclesmagazine.org
Gerald Jampolsky – *Love is Letting Go of Fear* – www.jerryjampolsky.com
Gary Renard – *The Disappearance of the Universe* – www.garyrenard.com
Marianne Williamson – *A Return to Love* – www.mariannewilliamson.com
Michael Mirdad – *A Course in Miracles I* and *II* (audio CDs) – www.grailproductions.com
Jerry Stefaniak – *A Course in Miracles Overview* (audio CDs) – www.innerawakenings.org

I am affected only by my thoughts. (Lesson 338)

Erroneous thinking greatly prolongs and strengthens grief. A time of loss is the perfect time to put effort toward learning and reinforcing ways of thinking that uplift and reflect the light of Truth.

Wherever you go, there you are.—Anonymous

Our thoughts are the operative constant in this humorous observation. But we can learn different ways of thinking.

> *You will need your learning most in situations which appear to be upsetting, rather than in those which already seem to be calm and quiet. The purpose of your learning is to enable you to bring the quiet with you, and to heal distress and turmoil. This is not done by avoiding them and seeking a haven of isolation for yourself.*
>
> *You will yet learn that peace is part of you, and requires only that you be there to embrace any situation in which you are. And finally you will learn that there is no limit to where you are, so that your peace is everywhere, as you are.*
>
> (Workbook, Review I, *Introduction*)

Using grief and loss as a starting point for healing, contrary to how it may feel, we are not "going crazy." Instead we are waking up. Elisabeth Kübler-Ross' classic five stages of grief are

---

[94] Published by the Foundation for Inner Peace, www.acim.org, and others.

contained within Michael Mirdad's five stages of the soul transformation process,[95] but Mirdad also offers a spiritual map for transcending the traumas and heartbreaks we experience, allowing them to lead us to our destinies of fulfillment.

Soul Transformation Process	Grief
1. Dismantling	Denial
	Anger
	Bargaining
2. Emptiness	Depression
3. Disorientation	Depression
4. Rebuilding	Acceptance
5. A New Life	Acceptance

Mirdad explains how our trials invite the transformation of our souls, and he reminds us not to resist, interrupt, or attempt to control this transformational process. Like any remodeling project, the old must be torn down before it can be replaced with the new. Key is to allow the experiences of emptiness and disorientation—pausing in "I don't know what to do or how to fix this." Only in this space of "I don't know" can we receive Divine Guidance. This explains why many people have mystical revelations within great crisis—because events humble them to the attitude of "I don't know."

The greatest power in heaven and earth is thought.[96]

Now it is time to take back control of my mind and understand that it is a *tool* to serve my true Self, not a force that controls me. I am the decision-maker (as Kenneth Wapnick so aptly describes it) and the witness, not the victim of the ego's spectrum of ghoulish thoughts that parade through my consciousness. I am in control of the gate of my mind, and I can open to the flow of God.

> *I rule my mind, which I alone must rule. I have a kingdom I must rule. At times, it does not seem I am its king at all. It seems to triumph over me, and tell me what to think, and what to do and feel. And yet it has been given me to serve whatever purpose I perceive in it. My mind can only serve. Today I give its service to the Holy Spirit to employ as He sees fit. I thus direct my mind, which I alone can rule. And thus I set it free to do the Will of God.* (Lesson 236)

---

[95] *You're Not Going Crazy. . . You're Just Waking Up! The Five Stages of the Soul Transformation Process* by Michael Mirdad

[96] (*The Aquarian Gospel of Jesus the Christ,* Chapter 84:22)

The soul of humanity has been using free will against itself since the literal dawn of time. But we can also use our free will to reclaim our rightful identity and inheritance as children of God.

Once willingness to forgive is established, ruling the mind is the key to practicing forgiveness. Forgiveness is a choice practiced again and again through willpower. Furthermore, the state of my mind today is the ultimate key to everyone's peace and happiness, for we are One in Truth.

I rule my mind, which I alone must rule.
Now would I be as God created me.
On my decision all salvation rests.
I have no cause for anger or for fear, for You surround me.
And in every need that I perceive, Your grace suffices me.
(Lessons 236, 237, 238, 348)

Despite all of this uplifting and empowering information and months of devoted and extensive spiritual practice, one morning my head was again full of unforgiving thoughts about my loss. Exasperated, I prayed for a clear and practical answer, which I received immediately:

Don't believe your negative thoughts. Let them pass.

Each of us stands in the middle of our own garden full of the most fertile soil imaginable. Seeds drift through the atmosphere all around us—seeds of thought. Some of the seeds will germinate into beautiful plants, flowers, and trees—all bearing the eternal fruits of peace and love. These seeds are called "God." Other seeds will develop into weeds of many varieties—all from the family of fear. These seeds are called "ego."

I am the gardener, and I choose what to plant with my *belief*. The fertile soil is my mind, the simple servant of the seeds I choose to plant. My belief, like a magic dome around my garden, allows only seeds of God or also seeds of ego to be planted and thrive. When I see a "God" seed, a loving thought, do I believe it? If so, then it penetrates the magic dome, is planted, and thrives. When I see an "ego" seed, a thought of separation, fear, guilt, or sin, do I believe it? If so, then it also comes in, is planted, and thrives.

Whether my garden is full of beautiful plants bursting with the fruit of peace and love, or choked with ugly weeds, depends on my belief, which I can change at any time. And when I have allowed a weed to be planted in my garden, I can transform it into a beautiful plant with my *forgiveness* because weeds are not eternal fruit. "Ego" seeds and their resulting weeds are just smoke and mirrors, temporary illusions in the field of God's loving seeds of Truth.

Don't believe your negative thoughts. Let them pass. Ask God to purify all such persistent, negative thoughts as anger and despair. They are not real and CAN be transformed.

. . . it is impossible that you be hurt except by your own thoughts. . . (Lesson 196)

Intellect is one of our false idols,[97] but Mind is everything. In a balanced life, the intellect is the *servant* of the awakened heart—that part of the soul that loves unconditionally.[98] My intellectual mind wants "answers," so I regularly supply it with the right answers. Bringing the mind to Truth, of course, is a major part of "working" the Course. As I healed my loss, my morning prayer was rich in answers from ACIM, reminding me of the path of truth each day:

> Beloved Father, I surrender this day to you that it may be a day of peace, love, forgiveness, healing, joy, and abundance. Lead me through this day, and help me to choose love now.

> You are but love and therefore so am I. I affirm that I am under no laws but yours: the Law of Love[99] and the Law of One,[100] and as your beloved child I am entitled to miracles. Let miracles replace all my grievances.

> I am willing to forgive anything that comes into my awareness without exception and without reserve. Let me perceive forgiveness as it is. I forgive illusions, not truth. I will forgive, and my pain will disappear because forgiveness ends all suffering and loss.

> I recognize that I make no decisions alone, so I choose the Holy Spirit to make all decisions for me today, whether they seem to be great or small. And I DENY that my past ego decisions can have any effects any longer,[101] as I SURRENDER all of them to you for healing and transformation.

---

[97] In *A Course in Miracles*, an "idol" is anything we value that is not eternal, of God and Love. Only the eternal is real. Therefore all idols are false.

[98] This is why art is so important to us. Singers, musicians, poets, creative writers, comedians, dancers, actors, and visual and other artists can pull us out of the intellectual realm into the spaces of our hearts where our true identity lies.

[99] The "Law of Love": to give is to receive. *"Today I learn the law of love; that what I give my brother is my gift to me."* (Lesson 344)

[100] The "Law of One" is another way to state that there is no separation; we (the Sonship) are all one. *"You can think of the Sonship ONLY as one. This is part of the law of Creation, and therefore governs ALL thought. You can PERCEIVE the Sonship as fragmented, but it is IMPOSSIBLE for you to see something in part of it that you will not attribute to all of it. That is why attack is NEVER discrete. And why attack MUST be relinquished entirely. If it is NOT relinquished entirely, it is not relinquished at all. Fear and love are equally reciprocal. They make or create depending on whether the ego or the Holy Spirit begets or inspires them, but they WILL return to the mind of the thinker, and they WILL affect his total perception. That includes his perception of God, of His Creations, and of his own. He will not appreciate ANY of these if he regards them fearfully. He will appreciate ALL of them if he regards them with love."* (Urtext, T 7 G, *"From Vigilance to Peace"*)

[101] *True denial is a very powerful protective device. You can and should deny any belief that error can hurt you. This kind of denial is NOT a concealment device, but a correction device. The "Right Mind" of the mentally healthy DEPENDS on it.* (Urtext, T 2 B 4) *Denial of error is a very powerful defense of truth.* (Urtext, T 2 B 14)

I choose the Holy Spirit with deep gratitude, with joy, with relief, and with every fiber of my free will. I choose the Holy Spirit to make all decisions for me today, and I open myself to Your loving gifts.

Father, help me let go of the desire for love, attention, approval, and appreciation. The world I see holds nothing that I want. I want the peace of God. You are my goal, my Father. Only You.

I am not a body. I am free. I place the future in Your Hands. I am an instrument of Your Peace and an emissary of Your Love. Thy Will be done, by and through me. Your Will is my will. Your Will is the only will.

Peace. Peace within me. Peace on Earth. Holy are we all.

_____ (Here I recognize my vision for the day and the future, and ask for help to achieve this vision. I affirm my goals as I see them, but do not choose attachment to my goals or only a specific way of achieving them. I also voice my prayers for others at this point.)

I will to perform *only* the miracles You would have of me today.

Thank You for all the blessings in my life. You are my Source, and I am grateful.

And so it is.

My thoughts construct the temporary life I experience—my garden—without touching my eternal identity as a child of God. This is why it's never too late for change and forgiveness, and why peace is so close.

Father, Your memory depends on my forgiveness. What I am, is unaffected by my thoughts. But what I look upon is their direct result. . . . Only Your memory will set me free. And only my forgiveness teaches me to let Your memory return to me. . .
(Lesson 350, revised to first person)

Thought is everything. God is thought. The universe is thought. I am thought. How I handle my thoughts must be very important.

I can be hurt by nothing but my thoughts. (Lesson 281)

Father, Your Son is perfect. When I think that I am hurt in any way, it is because I have forgotten who I am, and that I am as You created me. Your Thoughts can only bring me happiness. If ever I am sad or hurt or ill, I have forgotten what You think, and put my little meaningless ideas in place of where Your Thoughts belong, and where they are. I can be hurt by nothing but my thoughts. The Thoughts I think with You can only bless. The Thoughts I think with You alone are true.
(Lesson 281)

The following lessons jump-start the day from the proper mental perspective and make an excellent lead-in to meditation:

I give my life to God to guide today. (Lesson 233)

I rule my mind, which I alone must rule. (Lesson 236)

Let every voice but God's be still in me. (Lesson 254)

Christ's is the vision I will use today. (Lesson 271)

My eyes, my tongue, my hands, my feet today have but one purpose;
to be given Christ to use to bless the world with miracles. (Lesson 353)

A Note about Medications

It is not unusual when one becomes clear that thought is the basic building block of life to begin to feel that medications may be an unnecessary crutch—especially psychoactive medications such as those for depression and anxiety, which may be prescribed in the aftermath of a loss. However, it is unwise to stop medications simply on the basis of an "aha!" moment. Until the truth that *"thought creates"* is fully integrated and believed by you in every cell of your body, at least as much as you believe in your pain, it is best to accept medications as just another manifestation of God's love. God works through medicine as well as people and angels.

Students of *A Course in Miracles* can receive treatments and take medications without being hypocritical. Simply:

- ♥ recognize that mind is the builder and the Love of God is the Universal Healer,
- ♥ surrender your dis-ease to God for healing,
- ♥ then, with gratitude, take your "medicine" in whatever form.

Therefore, if you were taking a medication when you began reading this book, you should probably continue taking it as long as you are medically advised to do so. In the event you decide to stop, follow medical guidelines for doing so, keeping close observance of your thoughts and emotions if the medication was prescribed to enhance or stabilize your mood.

Pause

I will step back and let Him lead the way. (Lesson 155)

Clear Quartz

Pause

I will step back and let Him lead the way. (Lesson 155)

Pause

Rest in the Lord, and wait patiently for him. . . (Psalm 37:7)

Sit with the emptiness your loss exposes. Don't attempt to fill this emptiness with some other thing (addiction) or avoid the hollow shape, or feeling, of it (distraction). In Truth, you are safe.

I rest in God. I rest in God today, and let Him work in me and through me,
while I rest in Him in quiet and in perfect certainty. (Lesson 120)

Refrain from making major decisions, such as moving or committing to a relationship, until you have experienced and thoroughly processed your loss. Let all things be exactly as they are for now. Pause to make room for your feelings and your healing. The angels hold space for you, and time will bend as needed to care for you. There is a way for you to heal, and with your intent you will see the way to healing open.

Listen. Listen in your emptiness. When the time is right, you will receive inspiration. Jot down these thoughts. Do the little things now; leave the big things for later.

In quiet I receive God's Word today. (Lesson 125)

I will step back and let Him lead the way. (Lesson 155)

Let every voice but God's be still in me. (Lesson 254)

God is the only goal I have today. (Lesson 256)

This holy instant would I give to You. Be You in charge.
For I would follow You, certain that Your direction gives me peace. (Lesson 361-365)

Pause. Let everything be in silence. Create a temple with your life.

Refill

I am as God created me.
I will remain forever as I was, created by the Changeless like Himself.
And I am one with Him, and He with me. (Lesson 112)

Amethyst

Refill

I am as God created me.
I will remain forever as I was, created by the Changeless like Himself.
And I am one with Him, and He with me. (Lesson 112)

Refill

In sacred geometry, God is symbolized by a circle, a graphic representation of All That Is. While the radius is necessarily finite, it is understood that the circle is really infinite. When another circle of equivalent radius is drawn, using a point on the perimeter of the first circle as its center, the vesica piscis[102] (also seen as "vesica pisces") is formed. The two intersecting circles of the vesica piscis symbolize God and His Son. Part of the Son seems to be outside of God, but this is simply an illusion caused by the constraints of concrete depiction. The flat, dense picture is an analogy for how our "departure" from oneness imposed limits on what is inherently infinite. In Reality, both God and His Son are never-ending; thus the second circle is always completely contained within the first. All that we are and all that we ever *can* be is part of the infinite circle of Love, sharing Its attributes.

As you heal, you exchange who you *seem* to be for more of your true identity, which is changeless and eternal. You can change your very matter (your physical, emotional, mental, and spiritual composition) to reflect more love and less fear by consciously drawing in the energy of Love Divine. Upon awakening and after every release (healing session, sigh, tears, massage, orgasm, etc.) spend a few minutes refilling with God.

God is but Love, and therefore so am I. (Part I, Review V)

I feel the Love of God within me now. (Lesson 189)

I am the holy Son of God Himself. (Lesson 191)

Imagine how you would feel if you *knew* down to your bones these above statements were true. From the list below choose a word or two representing aspects or facets of,[103] or synonyms for God and breathe them into your being, practicing the meditative refilling process taught by Michael Mirdad.

Peace	Healing	Wholeness
Love	Forgiveness	Hope
Self-worth	Joy	Bliss
Safety	Clarity	

Now, while sitting or lying comfortably with eyes closed and spine straight, refill meditatively using the following method:

---

[102] The title page of each chapter in this book includes a vesica piscis formed from two lavender circles.

[103] God, being One, cannot truly have aspects or facets. But in the world of illusion there seem to be several qualities that describe God. They are all the same, and all beyond description, but these nuances of language can help us reunite what we believe has been shattered.

Inhale: As you inhale into your heart center (or chakra), repeat the chosen words to yourself, feeling their meaning. You are drawing these qualities from God and the Heavens through the top of your head (crown chakra) down into your heart. Then pause and hold your breath for just a moment, as if to implant the essence of the words in your heart. This pause accomplishes "anchoring" of the energy.

Exhale: As you exhale, spread the essence of the chosen words to every cell of your body while you silently affirm "and so it is."

Repeat the inhale/exhale cycle (above) about 12 times.

With every breath you take you internalize and strengthen who you believe you are at that moment. Refilling is just formalizing this process you do unconsciously all the time, but making sure you affirm the ultimate positive—your holiness as a child of God. Refill with intent and conviction, feeling the full force of your true identity (the peace, love, self-worth, etc.) that you have chosen for replenishment.

Living in your true identity is energizing. Maintain this renewed energy by practicing balance in all aspects of your daily life. Refill further by cultivating comfort, peace, and beauty in your consciousness and surroundings. Choose happiness at every opportunity. As you practice releasing and refilling, you will discover an increased capacity for happiness, service, and choosing love now.

I am the holy Son of God Himself.
I cannot suffer, cannot be in pain;
I cannot suffer loss, nor fail to do all that salvation asks. (Lesson 191)

I am God's Son, complete and healed and whole, shining in the reflection of His Love. In me is His creation sanctified and guaranteed eternal life. In me is love perfected, fear impossible, and joy established without opposite. I am the holy home of God Himself. I am the Heaven where His Love resides. I am His holy Sinlessness Itself, for in my purity abides His Own.

(Workbook, Part II, 14. "*What am I?*")

Balance

Balance is the sustenance of peace.

Rhodocrosite

Balance

Balance is the sustenance of peace.

Balance

In my experience, after the quality of open-mindedness, balance is the most important thing. If we neglect our physicality, we are less able to do the work of our calling. If we ignore our emotional wounds, we cannot clear space in ourselves for higher consciousness. If we deny the importance of mental ability, we will make poor choices. And if we are closed to our fundamental spiritual nature, we will not practice complete forgiveness.

What pulls us out of balance? Is it not the idea that there is something we MUST do? "I *need* to get A's in school." "I *need* the latest clothes and gadgets." "I *need* to check my child's homework." "I *need* to not make waves in my marriage, or in this friendship, or at work." "I *need* to make *x* dollars." "I *need* to work harder than others so I will get the promotion." "I *need* to weigh *x* pounds." "I *need*: to do anything in *x* amount of time, to be married, to have a child, to own a house, to make this trip, to have *x* in my life, to know what's in the news today, to own *x* or *y* or *z*. . ." Our *"needs"* are utterly exhausting.

Believing in certain *necessities* lures us out of balance as we strive to make them happen. "I know I should exercise, but I *need* to excel in my job and care for my children to my standards." When I believe I'm compelled by necessity, I believe I'm a victim. When I understand I am choosing, I understand I am a creator. I understand that I am free.

I need do nothing.[104]

We do not need to *earn* our worthiness in the eyes of God. We are infinitely valuable and loved before we ever *do* anything. We need nothing outside of ourselves to be happy because love, peace, and joy are our birthright.

> *When peace comes at last to those who wrestle with temptation and fight against the giving in to sin; when the light comes at last into the mind given to contemplation; or when the goal is finally achieved by anyone, it always comes with just one happy realization; "I need do nothing."*
>
> (Text, Chapter 18:VII.5.7)

We don't *need* to do all the things we do—we *choose* to do them for various reasons that all boil down to the same one. We do what we do because we are not happy with the alternative. For example, we *choose* to go to work because we might believe in it, perhaps are fulfilled by it, maybe even love it, AND we value keeping our word, AND we don't want to be penniless "bums" and let our children starve, AND we don't know what else to do. We are not happy with the outcome that manifests if we do not go to work.

We have the freedom to choose differently and create a different experience. We *could* choose not to work and let that experience unfold—our *own* experience of "not work" given the circumstances of our lives. Even if everything we do is motivated by unconditional love, we act

---

[104] *Save time for me by only this one preparation, and practice doing nothing else. "I need do nothing" is a statement of allegiance, a truly undivided loyalty. Believe it for just one instant, and you will accomplish more than is given to a century of contemplation, or of struggle against temptation.* (Text, Chapter 18:VII,6:6-8)

unconditionally loving because we have *chosen* to listen to the voice of the Holy Spirit and not the voice of the ego. We don't *need* to do things; we *choose* to do them.

Practicing the idea of "*I need do nothing*" in our lives opens the door wide to balance. It's not a lazy or spineless (or even enlightened) decision to *do* nothing; it's an understanding that everything we do is a choice. "*I need do nothing*" is an attitude of peace. The urgent edge of necessity is gone, and we understand we are exercising our free will and creative nature.

Free Sailing

To choose love now requires a balance of focus and open-mindedness. With the awareness that God works through all people and situations, we must remain open to God's gifts and direction in the events of our everyday lives, as well as during times of prayer and meditation. At the same time we must retain focus on the objectives we already have, adopted through consciousness and inspiration, not default. Focused, we do not scatter ourselves by following every path that opens up, trying all suggestions, attending every workshop, learning every technique, or even reading every "inspirational" email we receive. Achieving this balance is like steering a boat in the open water—we recognize there is some "play" in the steering process and simply go with it, keeping an eye on where we're headed. Small over-compensations port or starboard do not distract us or keep us from our destination. We are focused AND open-minded.

The Earthquake of Change

The feeling of loss can tip us over. Even in a balanced life, the sense of loss makes voids that may threaten our stability, like shifting sands under a foundation. In an unbalanced life, loss can cause the whole structure to tumble or implode. Although dramatic changes may ultimately be for the best, they can be uncomfortable. It may feel better to dismantle in an orderly way than to have one's life washed away in a tidal wave. Yet both dramatic and orderly dismantling clear the way for healing.

Part of healing loss is establishing (or reestablishing) the balance that sets a strong foundation for today and the future that extends from today. Balance is the antidote to addictive patterns. Living in balance invites more gentle and orderly dismantling, and lays a strong foundational grid for eventual rebuilding. And since nothing of this world is permanent, somehow—somewhere—rebuilding is certain.

Therefore, despite your pain, maintain or begin practicing balance—physical, emotional, intellectual, and spiritual balance. Resist that which would allow your grief to pull your life even further awry. Keep exercising or, if you haven't been, start some gentle physical activity (with your health practitioner's blessing). Perhaps you've been maintaining a strong facade. Then relax and allow your emotions to surface and flow responsibly. If you've been immersed in the details of researching an illness or treatment, set intellectual study aside and nourish your faith. Make an intuitive choice, without intellect. Practice letting go as you take in a silly comedy. Conversely, you may have avoided taking a good, hard look at the facts of your situation. In that case, do so—with God at your side.

The Debut of Love's Child

If you have abandoned God while "taking care of" a crisis, prayerfully turn everything back over to Divine Governance. If you have, up until now, neglected your spiritual life, your loss is a wakeup call—an engraved invitation to the grand gala where you can remember that you are a spiritual being. Honor the debutante. Denial of your spirituality denies your true nature, and thus will always cause pain. Embracing your spiritual nature nurtures the only balance that is unshakeable. There is no true healing or joy until you claim your identity as the child of Love.

> *It is not YOU that is so vulnerable and open to attack that just a word, a little whisper that you do not like, a circumstance that suits you not, or an event that you did not anticipate upsets your world, and hurls it into chaos. Truth is not frail. Illusions leave it perfectly unmoved and undisturbed. But specialness* [what is perceived as unique and positive in the world] *is NOT the truth in you. IT can be thrown off balance by ANYTHING. What rests on nothing NEVER can be stable. However large and over-blown it SEEMS to be, it still must rock and turn and whirl about with every breeze.* (Urtext, T 24 D 3)

Fixer Uppers

Programs of improvement, while extremely useful and worthwhile, can actually lure us out of balance. We may "work on our recovery" and neglect our physical bodies. We may go on a diet and exercise regimen, and ignore our spiritual and/or intellectual natures. We may focus on studies and sidestep our emotional issues. We may work on "achieving" and forget about balancing. We may even become "spiritual" and deny everything else, including our need to heal.

Therefore, don't let any program—physical, emotional, or mental—over-take your life. Healing loss establishes inner peace. *Balance* is the sustenance of peace. If peace is a baby dove and love is the nest, balance is the branch, the mama, and the worm. Properly fed and sheltered, peace thrives to one day fly freely and joyfully. Integrate the idea that you are a spiritual being having an earthly experience, and *use* whatever programs you need to bring your earthly experience more into balance with your God-given spiritual nature. Build your peace by nurturing the God within, not just by following the dictates of a "self-improvement" program, which makes its goal your god.

Addiction in full bloom can be so big and omnipresent as to assume the identity of the addict. It can be as dramatic as possession. Any degree of addiction is spiritually serious, as it *is* an attempt to substitute the object of addiction for God. Some addictions can quickly end or diminish your life, closing the opportunity to do the work to heal the core issues the addiction is designed to hide. If you have developed one of such blatant addictions (alcohol, cigarettes, food, drugs, sex, gambling, to name a few) that can trample a path of unmistakable destruction through your life, embrace fully the program that your brothers have used to release themselves. Follow that program to whatever extent and for as long as is necessary to free yourself. Make the program your temporary god, if that's what you need to save your life. You may even find your service work in such a program. But NEVER let your addiction, or the program that saved you, define who you are. Do not mistake any addiction for your identity because you, dear child of God, are so very much more.

Balance evokes qualities of eternity—ease, longevity, continuity, and peace—and eternity is truth. To be maximally effective, God's messengers of Oneness need to embody physical, emotional, mental, and spiritual wholeness. This wholeness is achieved through balance.

Comfort

You do not walk alone. God's angels hover near and all about.
His Love surrounds you, and of this be sure; that I will never leave you comfortless.
(Workbook Epilogue)

Aventurine

Comfort

You do not walk alone. God's angels hover near and all about.
His Love surrounds you, and of this be sure; that I will never leave you comfortless.

Comfort

You do not walk alone. God's angels hover near and all about.
His Love surrounds you, and of this be sure; that I will never leave you comfortless.[105]

Through spiritual understanding and practice we learn to take comfort in the Truth: All is One, God is the only Reality, God is only Love, we are created in the image of God as extensions of His Love, and we have never left nor damaged God, nor He us. We have no needs. In the moments that we forget, Angels of Light are ready to comfort us[106] as we sleepwalk through the nightmare of separation from God in denial of our true identity. There is comfort for us amidst all the myriad forms the idea of separation manifests on Earth.

I call upon God's Name and on my own. (Lesson 183)

God's Name is holy, but no holier than yours. To call upon His Name is but to call upon your own. A father gives his son his name, and thus identifies the son with him. His brothers share his name, and thus are they united in a bond to which they turn for their identity. Your Father's Name reminds you who you are, even within a world which does not know; even though you have not remembered it.

God's Name can not be heard without response, nor said without an echo in the mind which calls you to remember. Say His Name, and you invite the angels to surround the ground on which you stand, and sing to you as they spread out their wings to keep you safe, and shelter you from every worldly thought that would intrude upon your holiness.

Repeat God's Name and all the world responds by laying down illusions. Every dream the world holds dear has suddenly gone by, and where it seemed to stand you find a star; a miracle of grace. The sick arise, healed of their sickly thoughts. The blind can see; the deaf can hear. The sorrowful cast off their mourning, and the tears of pain are dried as happy laughter comes to bless the world.

(Lesson 183)

Comfort is a choice—*allowing* comfort through your choices AND *choosing* to be comfortable with what is. Affirm that you are comforted spiritually by providing comfort for your earthly self whenever possible. Wear comfortable clothes, sit comfortably, don't overwork, eat healthful food you *like,* and allow yourself time to play, exercise, and rest. In addition, read, listen to, and watch material that brings you peace and comfort. Now is not the time to sacrifice, deny yourself, and drive and strive for outer goals that are not absolutely necessary. Be gentle with yourself.

---

[105] (Workbook Epilogue)

[106] Kuan Yin, the Bodhisattva of Compassion, of the Buddhist tradition, for example.

The holy instant is the miracle's abiding-place. From there, each one is born into this world, as witness to a state of mind which has TRANSCENDED conflict, and has reached to peace. It carries comfort from the place of peace into the battle-ground, and DEMONSTRATES that war has no effects. For all the hurt that war has sought to bring; the broken bodies and the shattered limbs, the screaming dying and the silent dead, are gently lifted up and comforted. There IS no sadness, where a miracle has come to heal. And nothing more than just ONE instant of your love WITHOUT attack is necessary, that all this occur. (Urtext, T 27 F 3)

Comfort arrives on the tails of our miracles of changed perception.

I rest in God. (Lesson 109)

Schedule regular bodywork, massage, or other personal services that uplift you. Schedule recreation and entertainment. Schedule healing sessions. Schedule a long soak in the tub, a lunch with friends, a leisurely walk, an afternoon with nothing "scheduled." *Schedule* these comforts to solidify the promise of comfort coming to you.

Jesus has promised not to leave us comfortless. But sometimes our focus on pain blinds us to the comfort that is available. Open your eyes and look around. What comfort is near you right now? What comfort are you not allowing? What comfort are you ignoring?

Several years ago I was with a group of people about to take a hike. I needed to change my shoes, and when the group took off without me, I felt upset. I was especially upset with the leader, who I felt should have taken up the rear to ensure that everyone was situated. I was so focused on my judgment of the leader who left without me, I failed to appreciate the comfort offered by the embodied "angel" who stayed behind with me.

The Children of God are entitled to perfect comfort, which comes from a sense of perfect trust. Until they achieve this, they waste themselves and their true creative power on useless attempts to make themselves more comfortable by inappropriate means. But the real means is ALREADY provided, and does not involve any efforts on their part at all. (Urtext, T 2 B 71)

I will never leave you comfortless.—Jesus

H.O.A.R.D. – Holding On Attempting to Relieve Discomfort

When we feel we have lost something, we are vulnerable to holding on to other things in order to compensate and ease our pain. Of course holding on to things only masks our pain for a short while, like giving a child with a toothache a teddy bear. When we hold on to too many things we actually create discomfort—for ourselves and others. Many have crossed the line into the obsessive/compulsive behavior of *hoarding* at a time of loss. So it's very important to be conscious with your space and belongings when you are feeling loss.

Is your comfort hidden in clutter and chaos? Then now is the time to clear away the surplus—whatever is excess, stagnant, and of no use in your life. Now is the time for housecleaning in all areas. Much has been written about clearing clutter and organizing your space. "Oprah.com" has some good practical articles on this subject. Peter Walsh, who understands the spiritual significance of too much stuff, has written several books, including *It's All Too Much: An Easy Guide to Living a Richer Life with Less Stuff.* Information is also available through the National Association of Professional Organizers.[107]

If your accumulation of things has become overwhelming, you will probably need help to clear out your space and organize what you choose to keep. This clearing out of physical things is part of freeing you to process the emotions buried underneath them, and it is crucial to your healing. A minister or counselor may be able to recommend a professional organizer. Another good place to look for local help is the directory of Certified Professional Organizers.[108]

Make your physical surroundings and body comfortable as an affirmation and reflection of the comfort the peace of God offers. Create the space and comfort to *seek the peace of God*, and you are already partway home, having secured "a line in a quiet office to make your call."

I need but call and You will answer me. (Lesson 327)

Of course being "comfortable" is not required, nor even necessarily recommended, as a spiritual practice. Even within the context of healing, looking at our own issues can be quite uncomfortable.[109] We may choose to live in austerity as part of our spiritual path. Many spiritual practices and initiations can be uncomfortable—vision quests, fasting, sweat lodges, long periods of meditation under adverse circumstances, and the like. When we undertake such practices, we are learning to overlook some pain and transcend the body and its "demands." But when we are in the midst of healing a loss, we are already in pain. I am suggesting that we let that pain suffice for the time being and not give ourselves more pain to conquer.

Seek the peace of God, and your comfort is eternally ensured.

> [The Holy Spirit] *seems to be whatever meets the needs you think you have. But He is not deceived when you perceive your self entrapped in needs you do not have. It is from these He would deliver you.*
> (Manual for Teachers, Clarification of Terms, 6. "*The Holy Spirit*")

We are promised that our needs in life will be met with supply. The Holy Spirit will manifest according to the needs of our soul's purpose. We will be perfectly taken care of. But these will not necessarily be all the things and conditions we want or think we need. We will not be comforted to a point that impairs our ability to remember that we HAVE no needs. Peace arises from understanding and trusting that what we have at any given moment is exactly what we need.

---

[107] www.napo.net

[108] www.certifiedprofessionalorganizers.org

[109] Keep in mind that this discomfort of healing is TEMPORARY.

So now return your holy voice to Me. The song of prayer is silent without you. The universe is waiting your release because it is its own. Be kind to it and to yourself, and then be kind to Me. I ask but this; that you be comforted and live no more in terror and in pain. Do not abandon Love. Remember this; whatever you may think about yourself, whatever you may think about the world, your Father needs you and will call to you until you come to Him in peace at last.

(Urtext, S 3 E 10, published as *The Song of Prayer*)

Be comforted, and feel the Holy Spirit watching over you, in love and perfect confidence in what He sees. He knows the Son of God, and shares his Father's certainty the universe rests in his gentle hands in safety and in peace.

(Text, Chapter 20:V.8.1-2)

Your peace is with me, Father. I am safe. (Lesson 245)

Peace

I could see peace instead of this. (Lesson 34)

Blue Lace Agate

Peace

I could see peace instead of this. (Lesson 34)

Peace

Have faith in only this one thing, and it will be sufficient; God wills you be in Heaven, and nothing can keep you from it, or it from you. Your wildest misperceptions, your weird imaginings, your blackest nightmares all mean nothing. They will not prevail against the peace God wills for you.

(Text, Chapter 13:XI.7)

No matter how things may appear, peace already belongs to me. If I am not feeling it now, peace is somewhere in my junk drawer. Let me clean it out, and find my peace. And when I find it, let me dust the lint off and keep my peace in a place of honor. Let me find a pedestal for my peace.

Whatever it is, peace on it.—Swami Beyondananda

Cultivate an atmosphere of peace in your home and workspace to complement and mirror the peace you are cultivating in your mind. *Spend time in silence.* If being in silence feels uncomfortable, do it anyway with a *Mastery Forgiveness Process* or *Michael Mirdad's Healing/Forgiveness Process* worksheet nearby (for processing if necessary). We often drown out our painful thoughts with noisy distractions, but in so doing we also drown out our peace.

*Life with Me is not immunity **from** difficulties, but peace **in** difficulties.*
*My guidance is often by **shut** doors.—God Calling*[110]

There is a place in you where there is perfect peace.
There is a place in you where nothing is impossible.
There is a place in you where the strength of God abides. (Lesson 47)

For you was peace created, given you by its Creator,
and established as His Own eternal gift. (Lesson 186)

Conflict is sleep, and peace awakening. (Lesson 331)

Are you ready to wake up and claim the gift of peace?

I want the peace of God. (Lesson 185)

In Lesson 185 we are reminded that if we really wanted the peace of God, and only the peace of God, we would have it. In Truth it is already ours. Often we think we ask sincerely for the peace of God, but are actually saying, "I want the peace of God AND I want _____." That "AND" *prevents* us from experiencing the peace of God already dwelling within us. We become

---

[110] Edited by A.J. Russell. In December of 1932 "Two Listeners" began sharing a daily quiet time to open to Divine Guidance. To their astonishment they received personal instruction from Jesus himself. These loving teachings were published as the daily devotional *God Calling*. www.twolisteners.org .

attached to fulfilling our desire. We may even forget the peace of God entirely, just seeking other things we want. Our desires are not the problem—in fact they guide us. But our attachment to getting that which we desire will unfailingly block our awareness of the peace within. Even excitement over "special good" things blocks our peace.

Jesus asks, "What do you ask for in your heart?" The answer creates a useful tool to reframe any desire we may become *attached to* moment by moment. When *anything* disturbs our peace in any way, we can simply ask, "Is this what I would have in place of Heaven and the peace of God?"

Do I want _____ or do I want the peace of God?

For example, filling in the blank:

- a peanut butter sandwich, this piece of candy
- to get someplace on time, this parking spot
- to win this argument
- this person's love and approval
- this attention
- this cigarette, drink, sexual encounter, thrill
- this material thing, this physical quality
- to be right about _____ (my version of the world)
- to be a victim, this grief
- to believe in guilt—my own or others'
- a life of distraction, pain and want, seeking without finding
- anything the world has to offer

At first glance, some of these examples may seem silly, until you consider how loud and raucous the voice in your head can get about the smallest things. When your egoic voice is "screaming" and "fussing" about how hungry you are, it makes sense to counter with "do I want a peanut butter sandwich or the peace of God?" You are not a body, and your spirit container, your body, will be fed soon enough in the grand scheme of things. So endeavor to develop the discipline and presence of mind to recognize from moment to moment that you are *spirit*, instead of allowing your bodily sensations, emotional tides, wants, and all manner of concerns about the material world to pull you away from your center, your true identity—where you are one with God in peace.

There is no peace except the peace of God. (Lesson 200)

If this statement is true (and it is), then getting back what I think I have lost will not give me peace. If it is possible to replace what I have lost and thereby feel better, that "feeling better" is not peace because it is not the peace of God. I have only gained comfort from temporary circumstances. But relying on anything temporary will eventually bring me pain because temporary circumstances cannot last.

Choosing the peace of God does not mean I cannot have things the world has to offer. It simply means I will have the peace of God first, regardless of what else I may have. I put my energy into experiencing the peace of God and let everything else be as it may.

I am not a body. I am free. For I am still as God created me. I want the peace of God. . . .
The peace of God is my one goal; the aim of all my living here,
the end I seek, my purpose and my function and my life. . . (Lesson 205)

I seek but what belongs to me in truth.
God's gifts of joy and peace are [my inheritance, and] *all I want.*
God's peace and joy are mine. (Lessons 104, 105)

Seeking peace, I find that outside events and other people are well beyond my powers of control. The only things I can control are the thoughts I choose to entertain, my beliefs, and the actions I take because of them. Thoughts come and go and influence me only to the extent that I empower them with my belief. My emotions stem from the thoughts I believe. Choosing peace then becomes choosing, focusing on, and believing thoughts that create peace, and choosing the action of forgiveness.[111]

You will see your value through each other's eyes. . . .
This is YOUR part in bringing peace. (Urtext, T 22 G 8)

---

[111] *When you have looked upon each other with COMPLETE forgiveness, from which NO error is excluded and NOTHING kept hidden, what mistake can there be ANYWHERE you can NOT overlook? What form of suffering could BLOCK your sight, preventing you from seeing PAST it? And what illusion COULD there be you will NOT recognize as a mistake; a shadow through which you walk COMPLETELY undismayed? God would let NOTHING interfere with those whose wills are His. And they will RECOGNIZE their wills are His, BECAUSE they serve His Will. AND SERVE IT WILLINGLY. How can it NOT be theirs? And COULD remembrance of what they are be long delayed?*

You will see your value through each other's eyes, and each one is released as he beholds his savior IN PLACE of the attacker who he THOUGHT was there. Through this releasing is the world released. This is YOUR part in bringing peace. For you have asked what is your function here, and have been answered. Seek not to change it, nor to substitute ANOTHER goal. This one was GIVEN you, and ONLY this. Accept this one, and serve it willingly, for what the Holy Spirit does with the gifts you give each other, to whom He offers them, and where and when, is up to Him.

He will bestow them where they are received and welcomed. He will use every one of them for peace. Nor will one little smile, or willingness to overlook the tiniest mistake, be lost to anyone. What can it be but universal blessing to look on what your Father loves with charity? EXTENSION of forgiveness is the Holy Spirit's function. Leave this to Him. Let YOUR concern be only that you give TO Him that which can BE extended. Save no dark secrets that He cannot use. But offer Him the tiny gifts He can extend forever.

He will take each one, and make of it a potent force for peace. He will withhold no blessing from it, or limit it in any way. He will join to it ALL the power that God has given Him, to make each little gift of love a source of healing for everyone. Each little gift you offer to the other lights up the world. Be not concerned with darkness; look AWAY from it, and TOWARD each other. And let the darkness be dispelled by Him Who knows the light, and lays it gently in each gentle smile of faith and confidence with which you bless each other. (Urtext, T 22 G 7-10)

I could see peace instead of this. (Lesson 34)

As I learn to cultivate peace in my thoughts, replace my fluctuating emotions with peace, and focus on peace, my experience becomes peaceful.

I am one Self, united with my Creator.
Serenity and perfect peace are mine, because I am one Self,
completely whole, at one with all creation and with God. (Lesson 113)

Your peace is with me, Father. I am safe. (Lesson 245)

Today the peace of God envelops me, and I forget all things except His Love. (Lesson 346)

Beauty

Out of your joy, you will create beauty in His Name. . . (Text, Chapter 11)

Moonstone

Beauty

Out of your joy, you will create beauty in His Name. . . (Text, Chapter 11)

Beauty

. . . When the light comes, and you have said, "God's Will is mine," you will see such beauty that you will know it is not of you. Out of your joy, you will create beauty in His Name, for your joy could no more be contained than His. The bleak little world will vanish into nothingness, and your heart will be so filled with joy that it will leap into Heaven and into the Presence of God. I cannot tell you what this will be like, for your heart is not ready. Yet I can tell you, and remind you often, that what God wills for Himself He wills for you, and what He wills for you is yours.

The way is not hard, but it IS very different. Yours is the way of pain, of which God knows nothing. That way is hard indeed, and very lonely. Fear and grief are your guests, and they go with you and abide with you on the way. But the dark journey is not the way of God's Son. Walk in light, and do not see the dark companions, for they are not fit companions for the Son of God, who was created OF light and IN light. . . . (Text, Chapter 11:III.3-4, *"From Darkness to Light"*)

The world around us becomes more beautiful as we shift our inner world, reclaiming the eye for beauty—the eye single for love—inherent to the Son of God.

Perception is a mirror, not a fact. (Lesson 304)

Although seeing beauty depends on our state of mind, still there is much we can do with our physical surroundings to support the inner changes we are making. Make the beauty that is yours visible! Clear out the clutter around you and organize your belongings. Take your "good" things out of storage and use them. Erect altars to beauty throughout your environment. Fashion a landscape that reflects from your senses back into your heart what is true—that you are enveloped within the Love of God and that beauty naturally crystallizes from this energy of Love into all vibrations our physical bodies can perceive—sight, sound, smell, touch, and taste.

The world will be saved by beauty.—Dostoevsky

Nurture beauty in your life now. Wear and use your beautiful things. Enjoy art and music—whatever you find beautiful—now. Treat your daily life like a special occasion, and do something you usually keep in reserve for company or an "event." If you love them, get fresh flowers—yes, just for yourself because it's today! Light your candles today! Pick up some of that special food you love. Serve breakfast to yourself on your best china. Have dinner in the back yard under a tree. Take a walk at sunset instead of doing chores. Bring aromatherapy into your life by wearing essential oils as scent, adding them to your bath, and diffusing them in your home. If you're having trouble sleeping, dab a little lavender on the inside neckline of your nightclothes or on a tissue inside your pillowcase. Indulge in a soak in the tub. Try a moon bath with Himalayan bath salts and a favorite essential oil, enhancing detoxification on the new moon and absorption of the abundant minerals in the salts on the full moon.

If you've been saving your "good" or "clean" things, start using them now. If, in your grief, you simply have stopped treating yourself to what you enjoy, make the effort to resume now. If you have lost all your belongings, or are living in temporary quarters, it is especially helpful to nurture some beauty in your environment now. The beauty of a simple tent can be revealed with cleanliness and order. Open the flaps, sweep it out, and let the light in.

Make use of light—sunlight, prisms, mirrors, colored bulbs, colored glass, mood lighting, gems, minerals, candles. Use light of all kinds to brighten your path now. The possibilities are as vast as your imagination. Experiment with strings of colored lights around a window or shelf, salt lamps, paper lanterns, night lights, specialty bulbs, spotlights, and lights behind furniture and in other unexpected places.

Again, pare down your "stuff," getting rid of items you can't or don't use. Don't hoard your grief by hanging on to "things." Give away or sell what can be put to good use and recycle or throw away what can't. Clear clutter and put things where they belong. Give yourself the beauty of space. Allow the beauty of your things to delight you. Make room for joyful energy to bounce and reverberate around and through you. Make room for angels to dance in your midst.

If your things have been damaged (by water or smoke, for instance), be selective about what you keep. (Consult with a restoration company for guidance on this.) Avoid keeping marred items. While you might make an exception for a very special photograph or book or statue, the rest of your salvage should be as clean and functional as before it was damaged. You are making a clean start, and your possessions, as extensions of yourself, should reflect that.

If you have lost a person through death, divorce, or break-up, do not surround yourself with their possessions or things that symbolize your relationship. Yet when a loved one has passed on, creating a small shrine (with distinct boundaries) can be very healing. This process offers an opportunity to feel your emotions and define memories to cherish. Artfully gather select possessions and photographs together in one area to honor the memory of the person they represent. Discard or pack other things away. For break-up situations, most photos should be taken down and discarded or packed away. You do not necessarily have to discard all of your mementos, but do not steep yourself in them and do not allow their volume to overshadow your life today. They represent the past, which is over.

Perception is a mirror, not a fact. So all that I see outside of me is a reflection of my inner state of being, both positive and negative.

In addition to evoking and enhancing the beauty of your home (which reflects your inner state), take time to appreciate the beauty of nature around you. In truth, nature's beauty *is* you. Yes, stop and smell the ozone. Witness the beauty in the sound of raindrops striking the earth and appreciate that the storm always passes. You needn't take a trip to the wilderness, just pause to take in the beauty of the cat, squirrel, bird, flower, insect, breeze, clouds, rainbow, or moon in your path today. Breathe in the beauty that you see, knowing it is a reflection of the beauty of *you*, God's Son.

> *Our hands imbibe like roots, so I place them on what is beautiful in this world.*
> *I fold them in prayer, and they draw from the heavens light.*—St. Francis of Assisi

Don't be discouraged by the things you see that do not strike you as beautiful. Be gentle with yourself. Can you see the opportunity for healing and forgiveness in them? Can you appreciate the immense beauty of *that*? Anything that isn't love offers an opportunity to heal.

The real world is attained simply by the COMPLETE forgiveness of the old; the world you see WITHOUT forgiveness. The Great Transformer of perception will undertake WITH you the careful searching of the mind that MADE this world, and uncover TO YOU the SEEMING reasons for your making it. In the light of the REAL reason which He brings, as you follow Him, He will SHOW you that there is NO reason here at all. Each spot HIS reason touches, grows alive with beauty. And what SEEMED ugly, in the darkness of your LACK of reason, is suddenly released to loveliness. Not even what the Son of God made in insanity, could be without a hidden spark of beauty, that gentleness could release.

All this beauty will rise to bless your sight, as you look upon the world with forgiving eyes. For forgiveness literally TRANSFORMS vision, and lets you see the real world, reaching quietly and gently across chaos, and removing all illusions that had twisted your perception, and fixed it on the past. The smallest leaf becomes a thing of wonder, and a blade of grass a sign of God's perfection. From the forgiven world, the Son of God is lifted easily to his home. And there, he knows that he has ALWAYS rested there in peace. (Urtext, T 17 C 5-6)

While out walking one morning, I noticed a lot of trash and litter. I asked myself what it symbolized for me in the context of wounds to heal and forgive. I heard "futility." I've never been much of a litterbug. Even when I smoked many years ago, I had a method of emptying my cigarettes of ash and the last bits of tobacco so I could stash the butts in my purse or pocket and throw them away responsibly. Thus it was hard to see the trash as a literal projection of the litterbug in me. But I could relate to the idea of futility, as I have often wrestled with the thought of giving up. I suppose a person might leave garbage around, feeling there is no other option or believing the presence of garbage is inevitable—thoughts of futility. So as I walked, I forgave the error of futility in myself (projected onto others who litter) and refilled with purpose and certainty. After I used the "ugly litter" to heal the part of myself that believes in futility, I "litter-ally" stopped noticing the trash!

> *. . . beauty is not a need but an ecstasy.*
> *It is not a mouth thirsting nor an empty hand stretched forth,*
> *But rather a heart enflamed and a soul enchanted.*
> *It is not the image you would see nor the song you would hear,*
> *But rather an image you see though you close your eyes*
> *and a song you hear though you shut your ears.*
> *. . . beauty is life when life unveils her holy face.*
> *But you are life and you are the veil.*
> *Beauty is eternity gazing at itself in a mirror.*
> *But you are eternity and you are the mirror.*[112]

---

[112] Excerpt from "On Beauty" from *The Prophet* by Kahlil Gibran

Stretch your understanding and awareness in all ways, including expanding your definition of beauty. Have you ever appreciated the beauty of a thick layer of dust on a piece of furniture, seen the softness of it, the testament to stillness? Can you see a piece of trash in the street without judgment and open to receive its message instead? Can you look beyond your own physical idiosyncrasies or signs of aging and see the beauty in yourself? Can you see the beauty in others of all shapes, sizes, colors, and features? Have you accepted and forgiven what you see in the mirror?

I will not value what is valueless. (Lesson 133)

Although outer beauty may be an indication of inner beauty, inner beauty is the prize to be valued, for it will never change. All things seen by the body's eyes are temporary. I value only the eternal and that which takes nothing away from anyone.

The treasures of the earth are but illusive things that pass away.[113]

---

[113] (*The Aquarian Gospel of Jesus the Christ*, Section XVI, Chapter 99:20)

Choose Happiness

I share God's Will for happiness for me, and I accept it as my function now. (Lesson 102)

Rose Quartz

Choose Happiness

I share God's Will for happiness for me, and I accept it as my function now. (Lesson 102)

Choose Happiness

Achievement is not happiness. When we confuse attaining some goal or having some "thing" with happiness, it's like deciding on January 1 that we will be happy when Christmas comes again. There are a lot of days between now and then! Happiness is a baseline state cultivated moment by moment, maintained through loving perceptions.[114]

The Course advises, *"Seek not outside yourself. For it will fail, and you will weep each time an idol falls,"* then asks, *". . . Do you prefer that you be right or happy?"*[115] The truth and usefulness of this question is easily seen in the context of a disagreement between parties. But its truth is equally applicable to healing loss. When we are feeling the pain of loss, we are insisting that *our* vision of how our lives should be (needing something outside ourselves) is *right* at the expense of accepting the happiness available to us now. Instead we need to open to God's vision for our lives, accepting everything as it comes. We need to cultivate the response of faith and trust, no matter what contrary opinion we may temporarily be tempted to hold about the events in our lives. In so doing we choose happiness.

> *As God created you, you must remain unchangeable, with transitory states by definition false. And that includes all shifts in feeling, alterations in conditions of the body and the mind; in all awareness and in all response.* (Lesson 152)

In Truth or Heaven or eternity, the bliss of changeless peace within the Love of God is our natural state. It is the *only* state. In the illusory world of form, on the other hand, happiness is a *constant choice* made in light of our changeless peace. Worldly things we think bring happiness turn out to be mere distraction.

> *Beyond this world is the world I want. . . . It is impossible to see two worlds.*
> *Let me accept. . .* [God's strength] *and see no value in this world,*
> *that I may find my freedom and deliverance.* (Lessons 129, 130)

> *. . .pain is purposeless, without a cause and with no power*
> *to accomplish anything. . . . It offers nothing, and does not exist. . . .*
> *I share God's Will for happiness for me, and I accept it as my function now.*[116]

As you pray, meditate, release, forgive, refill, and heal, and cultivate balance, comfort, peace, and beauty in your life, you are choosing happiness. Happiness is being within sight of bliss.

---

[114] *. . . When man made the ego, God placed in him the call of joy. This call is so strong that the ego always dissolves at its sound. That is why you can choose to listen to two voices within you. One you made yourself, and that one is not of God. But the other is given you by God, Who asks you only to listen to it. The Holy Spirit IS in you in a very literal sense. It is the voice that calls you back to where you were before and will be again. It is possible even in this world to hear ONLY that voice and no other. It takes effort and great willingness to learn.* (Urtext, T 5 C 10-11, T 5 D 1)

[115] (Text, Chapter 29:VII.1) *"Be glad that you are told where happiness abides, and seek no longer elsewhere."*

[116] (Lesson 102)

Choosing happiness is remembering what Love feels like and keeping Love at the "top of the list." Nurturing balance, comfort, peace, and beauty in the life of your body will feed happiness, but ultimately happiness is a state of mind, not of form.

Aloha – To love is to be happy with.
—Hawaiian Shamanic Principle[117]

Practicing forgiveness and choosing love now is choosing happiness.

God's Will is your salvation. Would He not have given you the means to find it? If He wills you to HAVE it, He MUST have made it possible, and very easy to obtain it.

Your brothers are everywhere. You do not have to seek far for salvation. Every minute and every second gives you a chance to save YOURSELF. Do not lose these chances, NOT because they will not return, but because delay of joy is needless. God wills you perfect happiness NOW.   (Urtext, T 9 F 1-2)

Heaven on Earth is choosing happiness. Heaven is the only thing I want, and choosing happiness now, regardless of my circumstances, will help me remember it!

Heaven is chosen consciously. . . . Heaven is the decision I must make. I make it now, and will not change my mind, because [Heaven] *is the only thing I want.*[118]

There is no necessary conflict between the emotional processing of healing and happiness. Granted, you will be dipping into the depths of your despair. But *healing*, accomplished by refilling after every release, lifts you out of despair and back into your natural state of peace, love, joy, abundance, and safety. Even bliss—the worldly version of Heaven—can be reached.

Listen. Learn. Do.

In addition to choosing happiness with your thoughts and beliefs, take at least one action to nurture happiness on a daily basis, no matter how "down" you may feel. Nurture happiness alongside the temporary turmoil of your healing work.

---

[117] as related by Serge Kahili King in *Urban Shaman.*

[118] (Lesson 138)

To build the habit of nurturing happiness, make a "happy do list" of activities that bring you joy. Items can range from the very simple (like playing with your dog or having a cup of peppermint tea) to the more complex (such as walking on the beach, volunteering for a favorite cause, or reading a novel). Be sure to include lots of simple things. Write the most extensive list you can, then do at least one thing from that list every day. Doing more than one is even better.

Shake it 'til you make it!

Because the physical vibration of movement and sound will help to raise the spiritual vibration of joy within you, do some combination of activities daily that both *move your body* AND *use your voice*. For example:

- ♥ Sing and dance to uplifting music (music that makes *you* feel happy)
- ♥ Take a walk outside and chant during prayer or meditation time
- ♥ Do yoga to music and hum along

During my grief I got the most "bang" (energetic charge) from singing and dancing to loud, uplifting music. It acted as a holistic antidepressant, raising the vibration of my entire being as sound waves bathed me from within and without. My first choice for "uplifting and recharging" on an emotionally difficult day is a routine that combines music, yoga, dance, and singing that takes only about seven minutes! My favorite music for this is the opening from *Ritual, Nous Sommes Du Soleil* ("We are of the sun. We can see.") from *Tales from Topographic Oceans* by Yes. Using a recording ensures that the energy of the music is the same each time, giving you a reliable "crane" for uplifting. Pick some music you enjoy and get moving![119]

> *Light and joy and peace abide in me. . . .*
> *I welcome them into the home I share with God,*
> *because I am a part of Him.* (Lesson 112)

Sound vibrations can be healing. Vibration (from whence we come) is healing at a primal level. Many creation stories involve music or sound, including this one from the New Testament of the Bible: "*In the beginning was the Word, and the Word was with God, and the Word was God.*"[120] The Greek word "*logos*" means "sound" as well as "word." Although soaking up the

---

[119] A few more uplifting music suggestions:
- ♥ Jon Anderson: *Change We Must*
- ♥ Journey: *Don't Stop Believin'*
- ♥ King Harvest: *Dancing in the Moonlight*
- ♥ Chicago: *Saturday in the Park*
- ♥ Santana: *Everything's Coming Our Way*
- ♥ Coldplay: *Everything's Not Lost*
- ♥ Here II Here: *Holy* and *Free to Love*
- ♥ Armand & Angelina: *Love is a Boomerang*
- ♥ Bach: *Brandenburg Concerto No. 5*

[120] (John 1:1)

vibration of music around you is beneficial, it is even more healing (restoring to wholeness) to use your voice in resonance with the music, making your body *an instrument of the greater vibration*. Now you are affirming that the most intimate part of your journey as spirit on Earth—the body that seems to contain you—vibrates down to every cell with all the joy belonging to the beloved child of God.

The late Glenn Gould exemplified this art of making the body part of musical vibration. An outrageously talented and eccentric Canadian pianist who so masterfully rendered works of Johann Sebastian Bach, Gould was notorious for humming and vocalizing as he played. According to Wikipedia, Gould vocalized more to compensate for the inadequacies of pianos, claiming that "his singing was subconscious and increased proportionately with the inability of the piano in question to realize the music as he intended." I believe he also vocalized (and swayed) to better embody the vibration of the music, to entrain his entire physical being, not just the mental and muscular apparatus required in the physical act of playing the keyboard. On some level he wanted to crawl right into the music, and to do that he had to use his whole body, including his voice. Glenn Gould literally resonated with the music of Bach.

In addition to your voice, entrain your physical being with happiness by getting your body vibrating with movement. Choose a practice—yoga, stretching with an exercise ball, dancing, running, walking—any form of physical exercise you love, and do it now.

Be "Some Body" or Be the Embodiment of Something Great

Running through my "repertoire" on the piano one morning, I felt so much joy as I played. I realized that I had done a "complete 180" on why I play the piano. It's not that I didn't enjoy playing before. But the way I grew up seeing it, the better you played the more you were "somebody." I was not "the best," and, in my estimation, I never played well enough. So I was always trying to prove my worth when I played. I was trying to be somebody.

The change in my perception came slowly and subtly, as I practiced the principles of Christ Consciousness set forth in *A Course in Miracles*. Somewhere in the recesses of my mind, my reasons for practicing changed. I altered what playing the piano was for. Sometimes I ignored playing entirely for weeks, engrossed in other pursuits. I started playing different songs, learning some popular music instead of the classical pieces I used to try to master. I came to be playing because I loved the energy of the song and some aspect of the piano part—not a complete departure from my prior ways, but a change that excluded "good" music that was nonetheless not very happy for *me* to play. Now I play to lift my energy and *be* the embodiment of the energy expressed musically.

Listening one day as Glenn Gould brought to life the third movement of Bach's *"Italian Concerto" in F Major* (Presto) with such astonishing speed, precision, joy, and heart, I also heard the echo of the egoic voice within me that wished *I* could play like that. And then I remembered—I need do nothing. I *already* can play like that. Glenn Gould and I are one child of God, and when I join with him as he plays, *we* are singing in unison the same song of praise to our beloved Creator.

As I choose happiness by choosing love now, all aspects of my life shift to reflect my choices. I wake up every morning rubbing joy from my eyes. I see the path to happiness in all situations.

Mother Teresa taught that happiness is our birthright:

We have a right to be happy and peaceful. We have been created for this—we are born to be happy—and we can only find true happiness and peace when we are in love with God: there is joy in loving God, great happiness in loving Him. . . . Be happy in the moment, that's enough. Each moment is all we need, not more.

(A Simple Path)

The Course teaches that happiness is inevitable:

A happy outcome to all things is sure. (Lesson 292)

God's promises make no exceptions. And He guarantees that only joy can be the final outcome found for everything. Yet it is up to us when this is reached; how long we let an alien will appear to be opposing His. And while we think this will is real, we will not find the end He has appointed as the outcome of all problems we perceive, all trials we see, and every situation that we meet. Yet is the ending certain. For God's Will is done in earth and Heaven. We will seek and we will find according to His Will, which guarantees that our will is done.

We thank You, Father, for Your guarantee of only happy outcomes in the end. Help us not interfere, and so delay the happy endings You have promised us for every problem that we can perceive; for every trial we think we still must meet. (Lesson 292)

Happy Do List

Make Amends and Let Go

I am not a body. I am free. (Lesson 199)

Sodalite

Make Amends and Let Go

I am not a body. I am free. (Lesson 199)

Make Amends and Let Go

As you heal, you may become aware of apologies you want to offer others. Seeking forgiveness is an exalted spiritual tradition, rooted in the truth that our thoughts create, and so, we must be part of everything that happens to us. Making amends honors the idea that all negative things seeming to be outside ourselves are our own projections to be forgiven. If I "act out" my reaction to you, I owe you an apology delivered in words and actions. If I perceive that you have hurt me,[121] I still owe you an apology for my false perception. My *unspoken* forgiveness becomes that apology. In any case, I am called to open my mind and forgive.

> *How do the open-minded forgive? They have let go all things that would prevent forgiveness. They have in truth abandoned the world, and let it be restored to them in newness and in joy so glorious they could never have conceived of such a change. . . . all things welcoming, for threat is gone.*
> (Manual for Teachers, 4. *"What are the Characteristics of God's Teachers?"*)

> *Know the truth but respect the illusion.*—Michael Mirdad

Even though I cannot truly hurt others, when it appears I have, amends should be made. Tread lightly through life and make amends for your mistakes as you go. Concerning mistakes from the past, make amends only as long as doing so will not somehow injure the recipients or others. Bear in mind that it can be painful to reopen the past, and the possibility of causing others pain should not be overridden by your need to apologize. Other people who may be affected are especially important to consider, as they may have no direct involvement in the issues between you and the person with whom you want to make amends. Do not confuse your need for attention and approval with the need to make amends. Inspired by Byron Katie and the Course, here is a prayer of guidance in this area:

> Help me let go of the desire for love, attention, approval, and appreciation.
> The world I see holds nothing that I want.
> I want the peace of God.

Sometimes the best amends is a life well-lived, a life spent choosing love now. Thus your whole life becomes a healing amends to everyone, including yourself. You are free to let go of the past. You bless and forgive the world because you forgive yourself.

> *I bless the world because I bless myself.*
> *God's blessing shines upon me from within my heart, where He abides.*
> *I need but turn to Him, and every sorrow melts away,*
> *as I accept His boundless Love for me.* (Lesson 207)

---

[121] Search your mind in honesty, and you are likely to find MANY examples of your belief that someone hurt you that you never consciously acted on. Of course, you may have acted out your reaction unconsciously, or with someone else.

Letting Go

Most of the time, most of us walk through the world "knowing" how things should be. My loved ones should love and honor me. When I get in the car it should take about *x* minutes to get where I'm going. My friends should be "friendly." My child should behave well. Gas should cost a certain amount. A restaurant is a place to get the food I want when I want it. My bank should protect my money. Elected officials should act in the collective interest. Ad infinitum.

I do not know what anything is for. (Lesson 25)

The Course calls us to open our minds and *let go all things that would prevent forgiveness.* To accomplish this we have to remember that we do not perceive our own best interests[122] and let go of the idea that we understand the purpose of things and events in our lives. We have to be willing to say "I don't know what this is for" about anything and anyone. I don't know what my husband or wife is for. I don't know what my child is for. I don't know what my parent, lover, friend, teacher, job, money, business, client, house, face, body, driving, this moment, this "whatever" is for. I don't know, but I am willing to know. Father, show me.

I am not the victim of the world I see. (Lesson 31)

We also have to let go of the story of being a victim—the very idea that we *can* be the victim of anything. The truth about us is not found in the parade of stories that seem to make up our lives. Instead we come to see that all events in our stories offer an opportunity for healing, scripted—like our nighttime dreams—by ourselves. And in that understanding we discover the endless well of love that we are.

I am in need of nothing but the truth. (Lesson 251)

Finally we have to let go of attachment—to people, to outcomes, to ideas—to everything that constructs the illusory world. We have to be open to truth.

When we step back and allow the Divine Purpose in anything to be revealed to us, instead of giving the ego mind free reign to interpret for us, we have chosen peace. We have embraced our true nature and aligned with the omnipotent Will of God. When we learn to let go always, without exception, we will live in perfect peace.

Letting Go of Control

Everything is love or the call for love.[123] Those of us who are controlling call for love in the form of intimacy, and yet are afraid of being controlled. The controlling person can't relax, enjoy, and

---

[122] (Lesson 24)

[123] *A call for help is GIVEN help. The only judgment involved at all is in the Holy Spirit's one division into two categories; one of love, and the other, the call for love.* (Urtext, T 14 F 7)

be himself without controlling the parameters of his environment, including people. He controls (sets up his comfort) to set the stage for intimacy, and destroys intimacy in the process. No matter how loving the façade (codependents[124] may acquiesce to control), intimacy cannot be present because neither person has allowed authenticity. Once the dynamic of control has been established, all those who *would* love the controller are instead self-manipulating in order to please or appease him. Thus authenticity in each relationship governed by control is destroyed and intimacy (into me see) is thwarted. Intimacy is destroyed whether the control is *persuasive* (people we want to be around) or *repulsive* (people we want to avoid). Intimacy is exactly what the controlling person craves, and controlling behavior effectively blocks it.

Forgiveness is the process for letting go of control. As a controller I must forgive others for seeming to have minds of their own, and forgive myself for fearing control and unpredictability. What sounds complicated is really simple as I give my life to God to guide, moment by moment, day by day.

> *Forgiveness is not mere sympathy, nor condescension, nor forced generosity. It is the ultimate declaration of equality, founded on the recognition that all crimes are the same crime, every failing the human failing, and every insult a cry for help.*
>
> —D. Patrick Miller[125]

*The universe is conspiring **with you** to awaken **you** and heal **you**.*[126]

One morning thoughts of resentment invaded my meditation. Recognizing I still needed healing around my perception of betrayal by the person who came to mind, I stopped meditating and did the *Mastery Forgiveness Process* on my issue. A few hours later I opened my door to a new client—who looked remarkably similar to the person who came to mind during meditation, with whom I had just done more forgiveness work! My bodywork session with this client now had a dual function as I offered the loving service of massage to both the person in the flesh on my table AND my estranged friend from the past. The universe gave me an opportunity to make amends.

I let forgiveness rest upon all things, for thus forgiveness will be given me. (Lesson 342)

---

[124] A codependent person allows things outside himself (people, conditions, and events) to determine his emotional state. He is dependent on relationships, even when they are unhealthy. He may vacillate between guilt for asserting himself and anger over sacrificing his own needs for others. For example, he strives to "make" his loved ones happy and cannot relax when they are not. He assumes responsibility for the actions of others, or excuses their poor behavior. He may expend considerable energy trying to "fix" things for others, or be reluctant or unable to express his own preferences. Codependence underlies a wide range of behaviors. Most of us are codependent at times. Many cultural customs of interrelating are based on codependent thinking, especially those around romantic love. Codependence is rampant in storytelling, creating opportunities for suspense, drama, and comedy.

[125] *A Little Book of Forgiveness: Challenges and Meditations for Anyone with Something to Forgive*

[126] *The Way of Mastery*, Shanti Christo Foundation. Emphasis added by Mira Carroll. Use of this material is with the permission of the Shanti Christo Foundation.

Make amends with *all* of the events of your life with no exceptions. While many of the unpleasant events may seem to be only the ego's handiwork, God the Omnipotent infuses everything with a pearl of good. It is our job to find it. With healing we can see that the past has afforded us all the opportunities needed to unveil the level of consciousness we have attained today.

> *If God said, "Rumi, pay homage to everything that has helped you enter my arms," there would not be one experience of my life, not one thought, not one feeling, not any act I would not bow to.*—Rumi

At peace with the events of my life, now it is possible to let go completely—to be *in* the world, but not *of* it. I let go of all my expectations and desires and accept what *is* in the spirit of peace and love. I let go and go home.

> *My home awaits me. I will hasten there. If I so choose, I can depart this world entirely. It is not death which makes this possible, but it is change of mind about the purpose of the world. If I believe it has a value as I see it now, so will it still remain for me. But if I see no value in the world as I behold it, nothing that I want to keep as mine or search for as a goal, it will depart from me. For I have not sought for illusions to replace the truth.* (Lesson 226)

Now I let go and live with my priorities in order, choosing only the eternal and that which takes nothing away from anyone.

> *All things are valuable or valueless. . . .*
> *I will not value what is valueless. . . .*
> *Heaven itself is reached with empty hands and open minds,*
> *which come with nothing to find everything and claim it as their own.* (Lesson 133)

Now I look upon the world with acceptance.

> *Today I will judge nothing that occurs. . . .*
> *I will not think I understand the whole from bits of my perception. . . .*
> *Thus do I free myself and what I look upon, to be in peace. . .* (Lesson 243)

Now I look only where my treasure lies. Only Heaven do I seek, and it belongs to me.

> *Father, I will but to remember You. What can I seek for, Father, but Your Love? Perhaps I think I seek for something else; a something I have called by many names. Yet is Your Love the only thing I seek, or ever sought. For there is nothing else that I could ever really want to find. Let me remember You. What else could I desire but the truth about myself?* (Lesson 231)

Process

All things are lessons God would have me learn. (Lesson 193)

Hematite

Process

All things are lessons God would have me learn. (Lesson 193)

Process

All things are lessons God would have me learn. . . .
Forgive, and you will see this differently. . . .
I will forgive, and this will disappear. (Lesson 193)

A lesson is a miracle which God offers to me, in place of thoughts I made that hurt me.
What I learn of Him becomes the way I am set free.
And so I choose to learn His lessons and forget my own. (Lesson 213)

Remember that healing is most often a process, not an event. How long does it take? It takes a moment, and it takes as long as it takes. You can always find peace now, in this moment. And then you may turn around and feel your loss again with a ferocity that brings you to your knees. And from *that* place you will find peace again. This is the *process* of healing, and it will get better, but it must be allowed to unfold. The changes healing brings are miraculous enough spread over time; there is no need for them to be instant. Be gentle with yourself and tolerant of the time you take on your healing journey. It is certain you will arrive.

Let us today be neither arrogant nor falsely humble. . . . It is not our part to judge our worth, nor can we know what role is best for us; what we can do within a larger plan we cannot see in its entirety. Our part is cast in Heaven, not in hell. And what we think is weakness can be strength; what we believe to be our strength is often arrogance.

Whatever your appointed role may be, it was selected by the Voice for God . . . [Who] relays it to you, giving you the strength to understand it, do what it entails, and to succeed in everything you do that is related to it. (Lesson 154)

Like meditation, the process of healing loss requires focus and return to focus when you realize you have strayed. Persistence, not perfection, ensures healing.

In returning and rest shall ye be saved;
in quietness and in confidence shall be your strength. (Isaiah 30:15)

Let me remember that my goal is God. (Lesson 258)

All that is needful is to train our minds to overlook all little senseless aims, and to remember that our goal is God. His memory is hidden in our minds, obscured but by our pointless little goals which offer nothing, and do not exist. . . . God is our only goal, our only Love. We have no aim but to remember Him.
(Lesson 258)

The Course describes a process of awakening to God's Reality through forgiveness. While it is always within the power of the mind to change instantly, most of us will experience many smaller awakenings in the context of our lives, slowly changing our minds until we reach the point of readiness to leave old nightmares behind completely.

> *The Holy Spirit* [the Voice for God] *mediates between illusions and the truth. Since He must bridge the gap between reality and dreams, perception leads to knowledge through the grace that God has given Him, to be His gift to everyone who turns to Him for truth. Across the bridge that He provides are dreams all carried to the truth, to be dispelled before the light of knowledge. There are sights and sounds forever laid aside. And where they were perceived before, forgiveness has made possible perception's tranquil end.*
>
> *The goal the Holy Spirit's teaching sets is just this end of dreams. For sights and sounds must be translated from the witnesses of fear to those of love. And when this is entirely accomplished, learning has achieved the only goal it has in truth. For learning, as the Holy Spirit guides it to the outcome He perceives for it, becomes the means to go beyond itself, to be replaced by the Eternal Truth.*
>
> (Workbook, Part II, 7. *"What is the Holy Spirit?"*)

As I have worked the Course I see that the process of integrating any of its ideas has five steps:

1. Understanding
2. Remembering
3. Practice
4. Habit
5. Integration

Understanding or comprehension precedes remembering to actually use the idea. Remembering to use the idea becomes practice. Regular practice turns into habit, and habit becomes integration.

This beautiful letter, from Jesus to Mother Mary at the time of Joseph's death, can be read as loving counsel to all who have ever mourned:

> *My mother, noblest of womankind; A man just from my native land has brought me word that father is no more in flesh, and that you grieve, and are disconsolate. My mother, all is well; is well for father and is well for you.*
>
> *His work in this earth-round is done, and it is nobly done. In all the walks of life men cannot charge him with deceit, dishonesty, nor wrong intent. Here in this round he finished many heavy tasks, and he has gone from hence prepared to solve the problems of the round of soul. Our Father-God is with him there, as he was with him here; and there his angel guards his footsteps lest he goes astray.*

Why should you weep? Tears cannot conquer grief. There is no power in grief to mend a broken heart. The plane of grief is idleness; the busy soul can never grieve; it has no time for grief.

When grief comes trooping through the heart, just lose yourself; plunge deep into the ministry of love, and grief is not. Yours is a ministry of love, and all the world is calling out for love.

Then let the past go with the past; rise from the cares of carnal things and give your life for those who live. And if you lose your life in serving life you will be sure to find in it the morning sun, the evening dews, in song of bird, in flowers, and in the stars of night.

In just a little while your problems of this earth-round will be solved; and when your sums are all worked out it will be pleasure unalloyed for you to enter wider fields of usefulness, to solve the greater problems of the soul.

Strive, then, to be content, and I will come to you some day and bring you richer gifts than gold or precious stones.

I'm sure that John [the Baptist] *will care for you, supplying all your needs; and I am with you all the way, Jehoshua.*

(*The Aquarian Gospel of Jesus the Christ,* Section VI, Chapter 30:5-19)

Ours, too, is a ministry of love, and all the world is still calling out for love. As we heal the illusion of our losses, we gain power to serve and join our beloved Brother in bringing richer gifts than gold or precious stones to the world. And He is with us all the way.

. . . let our minds be healed, that we may carry healing to the world. . . .
. . . [let] only truth . . . occupy our minds. . . .
When I am healed I am not healed alone. (Lesson 137)

Healing loss is a process hastened by focus and practice, but we are assured that we *will* heal and claim the joy that is our birthright. Free will allows us to choose the time we claim our healing and joy. Why not now? Our sense of loss is only an illusion based on illusions—a wisp of fog dissolving in the rising sun.

I can elect to change all thoughts that hurt. (Lesson 284)

Loss is not loss when properly perceived. Pain is impossible. There is no grief with any cause at all. And suffering of any kind is nothing but a dream. This is the truth, at first to be but said and then repeated many times; and next to be accepted as but partly true, with many reservations. Then to be considered seriously more and more, and finally accepted as the truth. I can elect to change

204 | Healing Loss

all thoughts that hurt. And I would go beyond these words today, and past all reservations, and arrive at full acceptance of the truth in them.

> *Father, what You have given cannot hurt, so grief and pain must be impossible. Let me not fail to trust in You today, accepting but the joyous as Your gifts; accepting but the joyous as the truth.* (Lesson 284)

One morning while doing my prayer work I remembered it was the birthday of a friend from whom I had become estranged. I decided to send her the energy of Love and Light, but as soon as I started, my egoic voice reminded me that she had betrayed me. I countered, reminding my ego self that her betrayal was only an illusion—my own projection of betrayals I myself had committed, presented to my awareness so that I could forgive and heal them. I had betrayed others out of fear of not getting what I wanted and believed I deserved. So had she. With this awareness of our shared error, my heart softened into compassion, and I ceased my judgment of both of us. *Then* I could continue sending her Love and Light. Healing work is usually a process. The benchmark of success is progress, not perfection.

> If at first you don't succeed, choose, choose again. Choose love now.

> *Trials are but lessons that you failed to learn presented once again, so where you made a faulty choice before you now can make a better one, and thus escape all pain that what you chose before has brought to you.*
> (Text, Chapter 31:VIII.3.1 *"Choose Once Again"*)

The Course traces all possible permutations of our dis-ease back to our own unloving thoughts toward our brothers in God's creation, and promises that if we bypass guilt and choose again in the spirit of Love, the Holy Spirit will assist us in healing by undoing the conundrum we cannot undo for ourselves:

> *Whenever you are not wholly joyous, it is because you have reacted with a lack of love to some Soul which God created. Perceiving this as sin, you become defensive because you EXPECT ATTACK. The decision to react in that way, however, was YOURS, and can therefore be undone. It CANNOT be undone by repentance in the usual sense, because this implies guilt. If you allow yourself to feel guilty, you will reinforce the error, rather than allowing it to be undone FOR you.*

> *Decisions CANNOT be difficult. This is obvious if you realize that you must ALREADY have made a decision NOT to be wholly joyous if that is what you feel. Therefore, the first step in the undoing is to recognize that YOU ACTIVELY DECIDED WRONGLY, BUT CAN AS ACTIVELY DECIDE OTHERWISE.*

> *Be very firm with yourselves in this, and keep yourselves fully aware of the fact that the UNDOING process, which does NOT come from you, is nevertheless WITHIN you because God placed it there. YOUR part is merely to return your*

thinking to the point at which the error was made, and give it over to the Atonement [forgiveness] *in peace. Say to yourselves the following, as sincerely as you can, remembering that the Holy Spirit will respond fully to your slightest invitation:*

I must have decided wrongly because I am NOT at peace.
I made the decision myself, but I can also decide otherwise.
I WILL to decide otherwise, because I WANT to be at peace.
I do NOT feel guilty, because the Holy Spirit will undo ALL the consequences of my wrong decision IF I WILL LET HIM.
I WILL to let Him by allowing Him to decide for God for me.

(Urtext, T 5 I 18-20)

Don't Be a "But" Head

One day one of my forgiveness issues resurfaced in my mind, and as I practiced the *Mastery Forgiveness Process* I realized my forgiveness work was being thwarted because I felt persecuted. My feeling of being attacked (of being victimized) built an obstacle to my *desire* to forgive, a mental "but" that interrupted my progress in that moment. I knew better, but was temporarily overcome by a victim mentality. I could not think straight. In humble sincerity I prayed, "How can I forgive when they are persecuting me?" I received an immediate answer:

Remember that it is only yourself you crucify—you cannot be hurt.[127]

"Of course," I thought, as I let go of my victim identity, "I am spirit and everything I experience here, save love, is a dream. I rule my mind. Regardless of appearances, I cannot *be* hurt by others and I choose forgiveness. I choose love *now*." In that holy instant I reclaimed my peace and the ability to forgive. And I can repeat the holy instant again and again as needed.

I will not hurt myself again today.
Let us this day accept forgiveness as our only function. (Lesson 330)

Healing is the most worthwhile activity in which we, the amnesiacs of enlightenment, engage our minds, energy, and hearts. Healing prepares us to embody Christ Consciousness, our destiny prophesied by Jesus:

What I have done, all men will do; and what I am, all men shall be.[128]

The journey to God is merely the reawakening of the knowledge of where you are always, and what you are forever. It is a journey without distance, to a goal that has never changed.   (Text, Chapter 8:VI.9.6-7)

---

[127] *It can be but myself I crucify.* (Lesson 196)

[128] (*The Aquarian Gospel of Jesus the Christ,* Chapter 176)

Trust

I give my life to God to guide today. (Lesson 233)

Turquoise

Trust

I give my life to God to guide today. (Lesson 233)

Trust

. . . all things, events, encounters and circumstances are helpful. It is only to the extent that they are helpful that any degree of reality should be accorded them in this world of illusion.
(Manual for Teachers, 4. *"What are the Characteristics of God's Teachers?"*)

God is indeed your strength, and what He gives is truly given. This means that you can receive it any time and anywhere, wherever you are and in whatever circumstances you find yourself. Your passage through time and space is not at random. You cannot but be in the right place at the right time. (Lesson 42)

So much for the notion that things are not turning out as they "should." The Course actually defines trust (the first characteristic of a "Teacher of God" and the foundation upon which all the other characteristics depend) as knowing that all change contributes to our good. If "The God of Love" is at the helm, how could anything else be true? It's not that God Wills or creates our "negative" experiences. Rather, God works with every aspect of the dream/drama playing out on Earth, ensuring that someday, somehow, good will come of each storyline to all the players. *"A call for help* [everything that is not love is a call for love] *is GIVEN help."*[129] Our trust in this truth becomes the only "defense" we need and the only defense that is not destructive.

If I defend myself, I am attacked. (Lesson 135)

[Defense] *gives illusions full reality, and then attempts to handle them as real. It adds illusions to illusions, thus making correction doubly difficult. And it is this you do when you attempt to plan the future, activate the past, or organize the present as you wish. . . .*

What could you not accept, if you but knew that everything that happens, all events, past, present and to come, are gently planned by One Whose only purpose is your good? Perhaps you have misunderstood His plan, for He would never offer pain to you. But your defenses did not let you see His loving blessing shine in every step you ever took. While you made plans for death, He led you gently to eternal life.

Your present trust in Him is the defense that promises a future undisturbed, without a trace of sorrow, and with joy that constantly increases, as this life becomes a holy instant, set in time, but heeding only immortality. Let no defenses but your present trust direct the future, and this life becomes a meaningful encounter with the truth that only your defenses would conceal.
(Lesson 135)

---

[129] (Urtext, T 14 F 7)

ALL miracles mean Life, and God is the giver of Life. He will direct you VERY specifically. (Plan ahead is good advice in this world, where you should and must control and direct where you have accepted responsibility. But the Universal Plan is in more appropriate hands. You will know all you need to know. Make NO attempts to plan ahead in this respect.) (Urtext, T 1 B 4ab)

Trust involves walking the fine line between being open to the Divine Unfolding and exercising responsibility and consideration toward yourself and others in your life. Successful "control" requires perceiving the greatest good for the most people and the ability to distinguish between "need" and "want." Control should generally be relinquished except when circumstances dictate the NEED for control for the greater good of all.

You can't plan an inspired life.—Tama Kieves

For example, if I need to keep to a schedule in order to accommodate appointments or simply get my work done, then I must ask others to be on time and stay within the schedule parameters. Controlling my schedule contributes to the greater good of all concerned. One might disagree, arguing that adhering to a schedule prevents receipt of the Divine Unfolding. But insisting on just "going with the flow" results in appointments that start and end late or work undone, rippling inconvenience outward to many. I may *want* the freedom of going with the flow, but *need* to honor my commitments to clients or coworkers. I am always free to choose to abandon the schedule in the moment, when I am so directed by inspiration or a new higher need or greater good.

On the other hand, I may routinely attempt to control aspects of my life out of fear, habit, convenience, and/or personal taste. Recognizing no NEED beyond the personal and not wanting to elevate my preferences to the status of "gods," I am wise to relax more and go with the flow. I open to the Divine Unfolding, for example, when I sometimes sit next to someone new, go to the restaurant another has chosen, take the long way, listen to a song I think I won't like, or look at the email I have already judged to be a waste of time.

I am asked to let go of the "vice" and vise of my seeming control of this moment, tomorrow, and yesterday and instead trust in God. Mastering trust relieves me of the burdens that weigh down my joy. Mastering trust allows my gratitude to flow freely for all that I perceive as good AND bad in my life. Mastering trust opens my vision to spiritual law, which I cannot see while entangled in the law of the jungle—fear, scarcity, guilt, and punishment.

I give my life to God to guide today. (Lesson 233)

In trust I can *relax* into not knowing what to do next and how everything will unfold. Relaxed, now I have a spacious consciousness to receive Divine Guidance on matters great and small. Choosing to trust and simply follow the path of forgiveness outlined in *A Course in Miracles* will lead me home.

Is it not He Who knows the way to you? You need not know the way to Him. Your part is simply to allow all obstacles that you have interposed between the Son and

God the Father to be quietly removed forever. God will do His part in joyful and immediate response. Ask and receive. (Lesson 189)

Ask, believe, receive. Ask, trust, and receive. Ask and trust. Into the future I walk with God, placing everything in His hands.

This day is God's. It is my gift to Him. I will not lead my life alone today. . . . I do not ask for anything that I may think I want.[130]
. . . I will judge nothing that occurs. I am in danger nowhere in the world.
(Lessons 242, 243, 244)

I know that God transmutes all illusion to serve His Purpose of eternal love. God works through all things for my good.

As sight [human perception] *was made to lead away from truth, it can be redirected. Sounds become the call for God, and all perception can be given a new purpose by the One Whom God appointed Savior to the world* [The Holy Spirit]. *Follow His Light, and see the world as He beholds it. Hear His Voice alone in all that speaks to you. And let Him give you peace and certainty, which you have thrown away, but Heaven has preserved for you in Him.*
(Workbook, Part II, 3. *"What Is the World?"*)

Forgiveness is an ongoing "practice" AND something to be achieved. Complete forgiveness is the ultimate degree of the practice of forgiveness. Complete forgiveness is boundary-free in complete *trust* in the Will of God and the Divinity of man. I know that I need only maintain my willingness and practice forgiveness. God will do the rest, working through the Holy Spirit with all elements of the illusion I call my life.

The Holy Spirit mediates between illusions and the truth. Since He must bridge the gap between reality and dreams, perception leads to knowledge through the grace that God has given Him, to be His gift to everyone who turns to Him for truth. Across the bridge that He provides are dreams all carried to the truth, to be dispelled before the light of knowledge. There are sights and sounds forever laid aside. And where they were perceived before, forgiveness has made possible perception's tranquil end. . . .

The Holy Spirit understands the means you made, by which you would attain what is forever unattainable [separation from God]. *And if you offer them to Him, He will employ the means you made for exile to restore your mind to where it truly is at home.*

From knowledge, where He has been placed by God, the Holy Spirit calls to you, to let forgiveness rest upon your dreams, and be restored to sanity and

---

[130] Changed to first person from *"We do not ask for anything that we may think we want."*

peace of mind. Without forgiveness will your dreams remain to terrify you. And the memory of all your Father's Love will not return to signify the end of dreams has come.

Accept your Father's gift. It is a Call from Love to Love, that It be but Itself.
(Workbook, Part II, 7. "*What is the Holy Spirit?*")

Making the choice to trust I become free to experience who I really am, the image of my Father, living in love and abundance. I am free to choose love now.

I feel the Love of God within me now. (Lesson 189)

Now I walk in a state of awakened communion with my Father, in vibrant peace and contentment, at one with the whole of creation and living in gratitude for all things and events.

My heart is beating in the peace of God. (Lesson 267)

Surrounding me is all the life that God created in His Love. It calls to me in every heartbeat and in every breath; in every action and in every thought. Peace fills my heart, and floods my body with the purpose of forgiveness. Now my mind is healed, and all I need to save the world is given me. Each heartbeat brings me peace; each breath infuses me with strength. I am a messenger of God, directed by His Voice, sustained by Him in love, and held forever quiet and at peace within His loving Arms. Each heartbeat calls His Name, and every one is answered by His Voice, assuring me I am at home in Him. (Lesson 267)

Perception is a mirror, not a fact. (Lesson 304)

If we have eyes to see, we will see symbols in our lives, mirroring our inner work, struggles, and achievements, and offering guidance. These symbols may be tangible things and events in our waking lives or elements of our sleeping dreams. Shortly after I began writing this book, I was given a tangible symbol of trust. A feral cat appeared on my patio. I fed her. My patio became her private domain and safe haven. She was curious about me, watching intently through the French doors that separated us, sometimes begging, sometimes flirting with her big, round eyes. She allowed a closeness that seemed reckless compared to other feral cats, and so I named her "Trust." But she was not so reckless as to allow me to touch her.

I started the work of coaxing Trust to trust me. In a few weeks, just as I was able to place my hand on her back while she ate, a parade of tom cats came calling, forcing me to humanely trap and spay her immediately. I would have preferred to wait until she became tamer because I wanted her to trust me and choose to stay, even after a frightening trip to the vet. I feared I had traumatized her too soon and would lose her.

When I released her after the surgery, Trust disappeared for about 24 hours. But she did come back and slowly began to trust me once more. Soon I again was able to pet her while she ate. She resumed sleeping the days away peacefully in her patio kingdom, completely defenseless just outside my door, an embodied angel and testament to the power of trust. And her trusting presence attracted another feral cat to the bounty of my table, one of the toms, a shy fellow I came to call "Miracle"—since the moment he changed his perception and decided my gaze was not enough reason to run for his life!

I was aware, however, that my petting was not welcomed by Trust. She tolerated, but did not enjoy it. I felt that I *needed* to pet her "for her own good"—to tame her enough that she could be examined by a vet without sedation, and perhaps even be invited to live inside. I also *wanted* to pet her so I would feel close, accepted, and loved. I imagined a day that I would cuddle Trust in my arms and feel her purrs of peace and contentment.

I knew my relationship with Trust mirrored a relationship in my life where I had repeatedly pushed too far and too fast out of my own sense of need for love.

I sought a reading of Trust from the Rose Oracle,[131] an animal communicator who knew nothing of my evaluation of the situation. Through the Rose Oracle, Trust expressed her desire to be close to me WITHOUT petting. While she enjoyed receiving the vibration of my energy and was fond of me, she 'said,' "No touching—it feels like shocks of electricity!" Trust said she had appeared in my life out of deep love and commitment, to help me resolve some issues around love, separation, and estrangement. She had arrived to teach me how one can be at a distance, yet still loved and loving, through the metaphor of a wild animal coming to trust a human being. She said that I should trust my natural ability to communicate with my energy and the love in my heart, regardless of the distance.

So I stopped petting Trust. Within a month she began to move closer to me of her own accord. After a couple more months she approached and "asked" to be petted! Then I knew Trust was content, and we shared love in complete comfort within the distance she chose, which varied. In this relaxed and trusting atmosphere, even her shy friend Miracle allowed more closeness.

Cats tend to be delicate eaters, preferring to nibble throughout the day rather than wolf down a big meal. To avoid attracting insects and other scavengers to her uneaten food, Trust was fed smaller portions twice a day. Since she chose my patio as her home, one of my daily responsibilities and mantras was to "feed Trust."

Seen through the eyes of intuition my experience with the feral cats is richly significant. God has invited me to trust and, just in case I need it, given me an example to study. Through my relationship with Trust, the cat, I can choose to see that I am loved. I can see that God cares for me and waits patiently for me to allow Him closer. This is true for all of us.[132]

---

[131] www.roseoracle.com

[132] I believeTrust, the feral cat, was one of the angels God sent to help me produce this book. She has left. I last saw her Sunday, February 13, 2011. She did not show up for breakfast Valentine's Day morning. My feeling is that she left the earth plane (in cat form, anyway) truly because her work here was done. I so enjoyed loving her, and learning the lessons she brought. She clearly demonstrated (as all companion animals do) that to give and receive are one. She allowed me to treat her for worms just a couple of weeks before she left. She allowed me to feed her and touch her and even trusted me enough to take a couple of good long looks at the world inside my home through the open door. She flirted with me in a mock battle a day or two before she left, doing that hilarious cat thing of making herself into an arch and bouncing around sideways before dashing off, just because she saw me walking down the sidewalk. She was playing with me—a true feral cat just "scrams" when people come too close. And she slept, groomed, and preened, hour after hour, a sentinel of innocence and beauty on my patio under the eye of my appreciation. She was a little glowing ball of furry peace and love.

Pono – Effectiveness is the measure of truth.
—Hawaiian Shamanic Principle[133]

In the big picture, everything turns out *pono*—in perfect order. All of my experiences are effective in leading me to the awareness that I am still at home with God. Whatever happens, will happen, or has happened, I trust my Father to use it to create a doorway to love. I can never really lose; I just temporarily lose sight of what is Real.

[The Holy Spirit] *seems to be whatever meets the needs you think you have.*
But He is not deceived when you perceive your self entrapped in needs you do not have.
It is from these He would deliver you.[134]

Let every voice but God's be still in me. (Lesson 254)

I place the future in the hands of God. (Lesson 194)

I need but call and You will answer me. (Lesson 327)

I will forgive and this will disappear. (Lesson 193)

[Forgive] *And God Himself shall wipe away all tears.*[135]
Where darkness was I look upon the light. (Lessons 301, 302)

Today the peace of God envelops me, and I forget all things except His Love. (Lesson 346)

This holy instant would I give to You. Be You in charge.
For I would follow You, certain that Your direction gives me peace. (Lessons 361-365)

God's peace and joy are mine. (Lesson 105)

~ ~ ~

---

[133] as related by Serge Kahili King in *Urban Shaman.*

[134] (Manual for Teachers, Clarification of Terms, 6. "*The Holy Spirit*")

[135] *And God shall wipe away all tears from their eyes; and there shall be no more death, neither sorrow, nor crying, neither shall there be any more pain: for the former things are passed away. . . . He that overcometh shall inherit all things; and I will be his God, and he shall be my son.* (Revelation 21:4, 7)

While working on the final edit of this book I dreamt of an exalted being. In an atmosphere of profound peace, this being told me personally how its "greatest" mistake or defeat had become its greatest triumph. I awoke full of gratitude, knowing that the message is for all of us.

I'm not asking you to sacrifice. I'm asking you to trust.

What incredible comfort these words bring! I am still staggered by the message—its simplicity, its depth, and the great peace it offers. Trust goes far beyond hope, for trust allows me to *rest* in the knowledge that everything turns out in the end. I need to control nothing, nor even know the details. I have not "sacrificed" or "lost" anything. Instead, many vital lessons are mastered as I heal my sense of loss. As I relax, trust, and learn these lessons, I find eternal peace and joy.

There is no will but God's. (Lesson 74)

There is no substitute for the Will of God.[136]

Trust allows me to choose love now and forges the way of the heart. What is the way of the heart?

> *It is a way in which you will come to cultivate—regardless of your inner experience or degree of awakening—the willingness and the art of returning to the simplicity of empty-headedness and not-knowingness with each and every breath. It is a way of life in which all things and all events become an aspect of your meditation and your prayer until there is established once again within you the Truth that is true always:*
>
> > *Not my will, but Thine be done.*
> > *For of myself, I do nothing.*[137]
> > *But the Father does all things through me.*
>
> *Imagine then a state of being in which you walk through this world seemingly appearing like everyone else and yet, you are spacious within. You are empty within. In truth, you desire nothing, though you allow desire to move through you. And you recognize it as the voice of the Father guiding your personality, your*

---

[136] (Manual for Teachers, 16. *"How Should the Teacher of God Spend His Day?"*)

[137] *Then said Jesus unto them, When ye have lifted up the Son of man, then shall ye know that I am he, and that I do nothing of myself; but as my Father hath taught me, I speak these things.* (John 8:28)

Believest thou not that I am in the Father, and the Father in me? The words that I speak unto you I speak not of myself: but the Father that dwelleth in me, he doeth the works. Believe me that I am in the Father, and the Father in me: or else believe me for the very works' sake. Verily, verily, I say unto you, He that believeth in me, the works that I do shall he do also; and greater works than these shall he do; because I go unto my Father. (John 14:10-12)

emotions and even the body to the places, events, people and experiences through which the tapestry of the atonement—the at-one-ment—is being woven, through which all of the children of God are called home again. . . .

Rest assured whenever you feel frustration and anxiety, it is because you have decided not to trust the Truth. And the Truth is simply this:

Only God's plan for salvation can work for you.

Your way must always fail. For your way begins with the illusory and insane assumption that you are a separate being from the Mind of God and must, therefore, direct your own course.

(*The Way of Mastery*, Shanti Christo Foundation)[138]

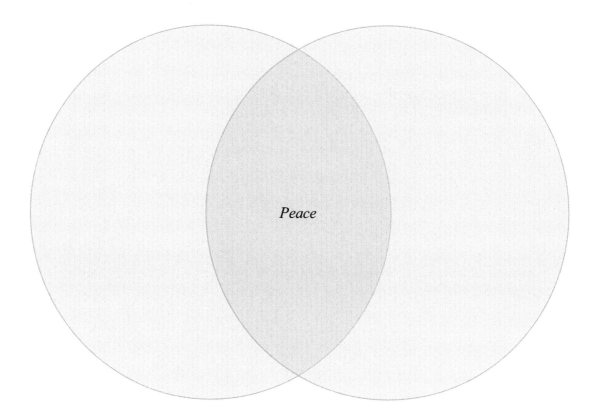

Peace

---

[138] Use of this material is with the permission of the Shanti Christo Foundation. www.shantichristo.com

Epilogue

Namaste, Dear One,

We are so very proud and filled overflowing with love for you and the planet. You have walked a difficult path with grace. Your heart is shining, and this increases our endless joy. You carry our energy with you—do you feel it? We are enjoying all the synchronicities along with you, although we are not surprised.

Please listen, and listen well. Humanity is called to let go of loss. In the collective it won't happen overnight, but for individuals this *is* possible. Letting go of an idea can be instantaneous, and loss is only an idea. As you go through the process of doing your healing work, remember that the whole concept of loss can be released in an instant. There is no need to "lose" again.

When it *seems* that you have lost yet again, cry your tears to clear your energy and refill with the presence of Love Supreme. Then open your spiritual eye to the holy gifts that remain and new gifts that have come to pass. Walk on in joy and gratitude with the knowledge that you have not lost at all. Do this, Dear Ones, and you are closer to home than ever before.

Things on planet Earth are not as they seem, and there is only one thing that can be used exclusively for Truth—forgiveness. As you have seen, all other things can advance the Will of Love or be twisted against it: love, devotion, feeding, sex, intellect, protection, happiness, control, freedom—to name a few. Practice forgiveness with abandon and you can't be wrong! Let *forgiveness* be your lifestyle.

We are with you always, and our names are not important. The rays of the sun have no need to be differentiated; they simply serve the light. We shower you with Love and shine Light on you and all blessed beings treading the path home.

With endless Love, in service to the One,

Your Guardian Angels

The Lord is my shepherd; I shall not want.
He maketh me to lie down in green pastures; he leadeth me beside the still waters.
He restoreth my soul: he leadeth me in the paths of righteousness for his name's sake.
Yea, though I walk through the valley of the shadow of death, I will fear no evil:
    for thou art with me; thy rod and thy staff they comfort me.
Thou preparest a table before me in the presence of mine enemies:
    thou anointest my head with oil; my cup runneth over.
Surely goodness and mercy shall follow me all the days of my life:
    and I will dwell in the house of the Lord for ever.

(Psalm 23, the Bible)

TOUCHSTONES FOR HEALING LOSS

Concepts and Practices to Choose Love Now

Forgiveness ends all suffering and loss. (Lesson 249)

1. Spiritual Issue – *I am spirit.* (Lesson 97)

2. Responsibility – I forgive everything because I make the world as I would have it. (Lesson 188)

3. Support and Service – *God's Voice speaks to me all through the day.* (Lesson 49)

4. Pray – *I call upon God's Name and on my own.* (Lesson 183)

5. Meditate – *In quiet I receive God's Word today.* (Lesson 125)

6. Pain – *Joy is just, and pain is but the sign you have misunderstood yourself.* (Lesson 101)

7. Anger and Forgiveness – *Let me remember I am one with God, at one with all my brothers and my Self, in everlasting holiness and peace.* (Lesson 124)

8. Past and Future – *I loose the world from all I thought it was.* (Lesson 132)

9. Emotional Healing Work – *I am as God created me. I am God's Son. Today I lay aside all sick illusions of myself, and let my Father tell me Who I really am.* (Lesson 120)

10. Mental Healing Work – *I am determined to see things differently.* (Lesson 21)

11. Pause – *I will step back and let Him lead the way.* (Lesson 155)

12. Refill – *I am as God created me. I will remain forever as I was, created by the Changeless like Himself. And I am one with Him, and He with me.* (Lesson 112)

13. Balance – Balance is the sustenance of peace.

14. Comfort – *You do not walk alone. God's angels hover near and all about. His Love surrounds you, and of this be sure; that I will never leave you comfortless.* (Workbook Epilogue)

15. Peace – *I could see peace instead of this.* (Lesson 34)

16. Beauty – *Out of your joy, you will create beauty in His Name. . .* (Text, Chapter 11:III.3-4)

17. Choose Happiness – *I share God's Will for happiness for me, and I accept it as my function now.* (Lesson 102)

18. Make Amends and Let Go – *I am not a body. I am free.* (Lesson 199)

19. Process – *All things are lessons God would have me learn.* (Lesson 193)

20. Trust – *I give my life to God to guide today.* (Lesson 233)

CRYSTAL TOUCHSTONES FOR HEALING LOSS

Stones to Assist Choosing Love Now

1.	I Am Spirit	Labradorite
2.	Responsibility	Azurite & Malachite
3.	Opening to Support and Service	Tiger's-eye
4.	Prayer	White Topaz
5.	Meditation	Smoky Quartz
6.	Releasing Pain	Chrysoprase
7.	Forgiveness	Kunzite
8.	Releasing Past and Future, Being in the Now	Rainbow Obsidian
9.	Releasing Emotional Baggage	Chrysocolla
10.	Mental Healing, Vision and Clarity	Fluorite
11.	Pausing in Open Inaction	Clear Quartz
12.	Refilling, Accepting Your Divinity	Amethyst
13.	Balance in All Things	Rhodocrosite
14.	Feeling Safety and Comfort	Aventurine
15.	Peace	Blue Lace Agate
16.	Seeing Beauty in All Things	Moonstone
17.	Joy, Choosing Happiness	Rose Quartz
18.	Making Amends and Letting Go	Sodalite
19.	Patience with the Process	Hematite
20.	Trust in God	Turquoise

MASTERY FORGIVENESS PROCESS

1. **RECOGNIZE:** I am the source of my experience. I am feeling disturbed. What *in me* needs to be healed?

2. **RELAX:** Breathe deeply and rhythmically. Let the body soften and relax, then. . .

3. **ASK:** What is it *in the energy* of this *person* or this *situation* that is really upsetting to me?

4. **RECEIVE:** You will see it right away: _____

5. **RETRIEVE:** Ask: When have I done that to another? When have I held *the same energy*?

6. **CONNECT:** You will receive an answer or a memory. Continue to breathe deeply and relax. Look upon the energy. Honor it. Love it. For it is your creation, coming back to you that you might embrace and transform it. Stay with the answer or memory, saying:
   - ♥ Ah, being _____. Yes, I sure can be _____.
   - ♥ I've been that way in the past. I know that energy very well.

7. **FORGIVE YOURSELF:** Looking with deep honesty and sincerity upon a memory in which you have been _____, say to yourself:
   - ♥ I forgive me for being _____.
   - ♥ I forgive my judgment of myself.
   - ♥ I choose to teach only love.
   - ♥ Let the image dissolve and disappear from your mind.

8. **FORGIVE OTHERS:** Bring your awareness back to whatever upset you, and say (to yourself):
   - ♥ I forgive you, (insert name), for allowing the energy of _____ to temporarily make a home in your mind.
   - ♥ Holy Spirit, show me the innocent light within _____ (person or situation in the present that you have found upsetting).

9. **SEE CLEARLY:** When you see the light, ask :
   - ♥ What is this _____ energy in them masking? What are they really crying out for?

10. **LOVE:** You will feel compassion, for it will be revealed to you why they are hurting inside. Sit with this compassion and breathe it in. Accept it as part of yourself.

11. **CHOOSE AGAIN:** Now you are prepared to choose compassion instead of reaction. Ask that God's Will be done through you, and your words and behavior can be different than you ever have imagined.
    - ♥ *For through you will flow exactly what serves them.*

12. **GIVE THANKS:** To your Father and your brother, for leading you back to love.

Michael Mirdad's Healing/Forgiveness Process

1. I recognize: (Describe the manifested version of the problem—facts, situations, opinions.)

2. I accept: I am feeling _____ and I am responsible for my emotions. (Condense down to the four basic negative emotions: **sad, angry, afraid, guilty.** Uncover the emotion underlying anger.)

My issue is greater than it appears; I have felt this way before: (people, events from the past)

This issue triggers my core soul issues of: (separate, guilty, afraid, unworthy, unlovable, empty)

3. I surrender the whole issue to You, God, for healing and transformation.

I trust You will take my upset from me. I don't know how to handle it, but You do.

4. I refill with (aspects or facets of God):
(inhale into heart center, anchor, exhale, and spread to every cell of your body for 12 cycles)
List Turnarounds of Step 1 here AFTER completing Steps 1-5.

Peace
Love
Self-worth
Safety
Healing
Forgiveness
Joy
Clarity
Wholeness
Hope
Bliss

5. I give thanks for the healing I have received.

Selected Sources

Books
A Course in Miracles – The Foundation for Inner Peace – www.acim.org
A Course in Miracles Urtext – Doug Thompson – www.miraclesinactionpress.com
The Aquarian Gospel of Jesus the Christ – Levi
Awaken From the Dream – Gloria and Kenneth Wapnick – www.facim.org
The Bible
The Book of Mirdad: A Lighthouse and a Haven – Mikhail Naimy
Crystal Therapy – Doreen Virtue, Ph.D., and Judith Lukomski
The Disappearance of the Universe – Gary Renard – www.garyrenard.com
Duck Soup for the Soul – Swami Beyondananda – www.wakeuplaughing.com
God Calling – Two Listeners, A.J. Russell, ed. – www.twolisteners.org
It's All Too Much: An Easy Guide to Living a Richer Life with Less Stuff – Peter Walsh –
    www.peterwalshdesign.com
The Kybalion – Three Initiates
A Little Book of Forgiveness: Challenges and Meditations for Anyone with Something to Forgive –
    D. Patrick Miller – www.fearlessbooks.com
Living A Course in Miracles – Jon Mundy – www.miraclesmagazine.org
Love is Letting Go of Fear – Gerald Jampolsky – www.jerryjampolsky.com
Loving What Is – Byron Katie – www.thework.com
The Prophet – Kahlil Gibran
A Return to Love – Marianne Williamson – www.mariannewilliamson.com
Still Here: Embracing Aging, Changing, and Dying – Ram Dass – www.ramdass.org
Suicide: What Really Happens in the Afterlife – Pamela Rae Heath and Jon Klimo
Urban Shaman – Serge Kahili King – www.huna.org
The Way of Mastery – Shanti Christo Foundation – www.shantichristo.com
The Wise Secrets of Aloha – Harry Uhane Jim – www.harryjimlomilomi.com
You're Not Going Crazy. . . You're Just Waking Up! – Michael Mirdad – www.grailproductions.com

Audio
A Course in Miracles I, II and III (CDs) – Michael Mirdad – www.grailproductions.com
A Course in Miracles Overview (CDs) – Jerry Stefaniak – www.innerawakenings.org

Other Writings
Miracles magazine – www.miraclesmagazine.org
The Lighthouse, newsletter of the Foundation for *A Course in Miracles* – www.facim.org
Edgar Cayce Readings, A.R.E. (Association for Research & Enlightenment) – www.edgarcayce.org

Personal Resources
Elizabeth Picone – www.elizabethpicone.com
Elizabeth-Hope – www.2believewithin.com
Emotional Freedom Technique (EFT®) – www.emofree.com
Mira Carroll – Free worksheet downloads available at www.alohaservices.org
Miracle Distribution Center – www.miraclecenter.org
The Rose Oracle – www.roseoracle.com

Artwork
Francene Hart – www.francenehart.com
Daniel B. Holeman – www.awakenvisions.com

Index

About the Author

Miradrienne Carroll began her journey as a healer as a psychology major. Her understanding of healing passed through several stages, from believing that intellectual understanding was everything to believing that psychopharmacology was everything. While studying the philosophy of the social sciences she became convinced that the realm of healing behavior and emotion is a subjective *art* that borrows tools from science. A bit later she was impressed by the fact that the majority of modern medical science recognized only one effective treatment for the scourge of addiction—the program of Alcoholics Anonymous—which is spiritual in nature.

Introduced to *A Course in Miracles* in 1993, Mira came to understand that the core issue underlying all dis-ease is the mistaken belief that we are separate from God. While many physical, psychological, and cognitive tools provide effective relief and support to get through our problems, *curing* or *solving* them requires a spiritual approach. This applies to grief, addictions, codependence, psychological and emotional problems, and everyday impediments to a joyful life such as stress and negative emotions. From this perspective Mira offers counseling to those ready to look at their challenges in a spiritual light.

Mira embodies a strength forged from walking the path of healing from depression, eating disorders, alcoholism, nicotine addiction, and anger issues. With the gift of sobriety, Mira transformed from a "seeker" to a "finder." Through *A Course in Miracles* Mira uncovered her crystal light and is polishing the facets through the spiritual practice of forgiveness. Along the way Mira has become well-versed in practical recovery, cognitive-behavioral strategies, hypnotherapy, Byron Katie's Inquiry ("The Work"), the Mastery Forgiveness Process and Michael Mirdad's Healing/Forgiveness Process, as well as transformational bodywork. Mira also borrows techniques from bioenergetics and EFT (Emotional Freedom Technique). Mira's approach is eclectic and intuitive, choosing the right tool for each individual situation.

Mira is an ordained minister of the Foundation for Christ Consciousness, a Certified Hypnotherapist, and a Licensed Massage Therapist. She is author of the book, *Healing Loss: Choose Love Now,* and her articles "Forgiveness 101," "Interview with the Ego," "*A Course in Miracles* and Mother Teresa," and "Independence Day" have been featured in *Miracles* magazine.

Advance Praise for *Healing Loss*

Ultimately it really doesn't matter what particular loss catapulted Miradrienne Carroll into the pain that hastened her awakening to Truth, for her loss became a diamond, which she polished into the uplifting and empowering beauty (for all to see and learn from) that is her book. As the teachers who have gone before her, Mira Carroll shows that for those who are willing to do the spiritual work, out of great pain comes great beauty; and as Keats wrote, "Beauty is truth, truth beauty." The overall effect of *Healing Loss* (the skilled intertwining of wise text, exquisite quotes from *A Course in Miracles* and other sources, and the magnificent artwork) is a gentle beauty that is encouraging, inspiring, and healing. Deftly and lovingly, Mira Carroll combines her healing wisdom with gems from Jesus and other teachers of healing until her book becomes a hymn to the eternal verity of our oneness with God that we can all sing.

– Rev. Lynne R. Matous, M.A., editor

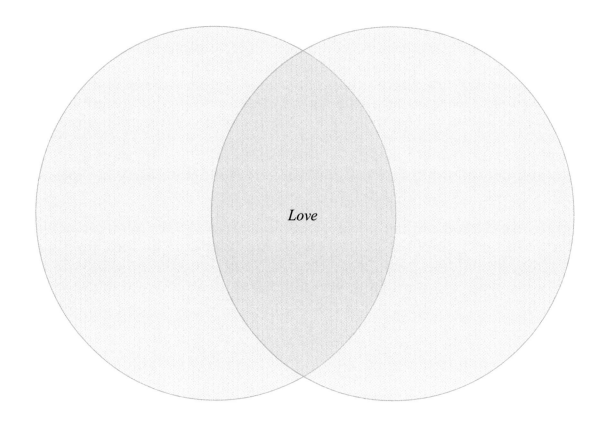

Love

Made in the USA
Coppell, TX
01 December 2019